California to New Zealand

The Long Way

by Marcia Heinegg

photos by Christian Heinegg

cover concept by Lenka Caraco

California to New Zealand THE LONG WAY

ISBN# 978-0-578-00143-2

Graphic Design by Staci Sambol, Slub Design.

To purchase a copy of this book contact lulu.com or mheinegg@cruzio.com.

Dedicated

to Family, Friends & Adventure

Acknowledgements

A Big Thank You to:

Ruth Campbell for editing gracefully;

Jeana de La Torre for punctuation editing;

Writing Journey's Friday morning writing group for feedback and support;

Laura Davis for creating an incredible writing environment and for her guiding light;

Women's group for support;

Chris, for the journey and the photos;

Lenka, for her love and cover concept;

Judy for keeping all my letters from the trip;

Louise for her eagerness to read each chapter.

And I am grateful for Staci Sambol's graphic design and guidance in bringing this book to completion.

Contents

Introduction

I am writing this memoir because I always wanted to write a book, ever since my early twenties. I attempted writing one about the San Francisco City school system when I substituted there in 1969. But a bestseller called *Up The Down Staircase* came out and I felt defeated so I stuffed the chapters in a box and put them in my parents' attic. I didn't know then that there is always room for many books on the same subject.

While pregnant with our daughter, Lenka, I took a writing class from Ellen Bass in 1978 and warmed up my old rusty writing desire.

In 1982, I co-authored a booklet with a friend called *How to Get A Job In Santa Cruz County.* It was a big success and it helped me launch my career as a job and career counselor. I wrote a career advice column for the Cabrillo College newspaper during the six years I worked there as a Career Counselor. While working for the Santa Cruz County welfare-to-work program, I co-authored a manual on career planning and job search.

When traveling with Chris to Austria in 1998, we visited his first cousin Brigitta in Graz. She was in her sixties and thoroughly engaged in writing her memoir. I admired her and a seed was planted in my head. My father-in-law, Max Heinegg, also wrote his memoir and I found myself reading it over and over.

A few years into retirement, I gave myself the old test: "Twenty Things I Love To Do." Writing was one of them. Coincidentally, I saw an ad in the Good Times for Laura Davis's Writing Journey workshops. I had met Laura when I worked at the YWCA as a Career Counselor in 1982 and she had come in for some guidance. She was then a student at UCSC and had a radio show on KZSC. She interviewed me on her radio show, and that helped publicize my booklet: *How To Get A Job In Santa Cruz County.*

I jumped on the opportunity to gather in Laura's class with other writers and write and read to one another. Laura introduced us to the book *Writing Down The Bones* by Natalie

Goldberg. That book inspired me and gave me confidence that I could write as long as I kept "monkey mind" at bay. At first, I was satisfied with writing and reading short pieces from writing prompts. Then Laura encouraged us to write the favorite life stories told around the extended family dinner table. The story of how Chris and I got out of Afghanistan in 1973 had been requested by my family and told many times, so I wrote it up, because it had the most juice. Traveling and then sharing photos and stories afterwards, is one of my favorite pastimes.

The following pages represent only six months of my life, but they were the most adventurous, risk-taking, outrageously fun, and mind-altering part of my life.

I've always loved the photographs Chris took on our journey and I used them as learning tools in Social Studies classes I taught in New Zealand. The stories are based on incidents that happened on the road with some imaginative fiction for seasoning. The photos fortify this manuscript.

I decided to sprinkle recipes into my book since I love food and cooking. I got the idea after reading *The Language Of Baklava* by Diana Abu-Jaber, a Jordanian woman who lived in New York and visited her grandparents in Jordan every summer and included her favorite recipes in her book. It's a delicious book and it inspired me.

I am writing because I like to write. I am writing because I like history and stories. I am writing for myself, for my own pleasure. I am writing for my family and friends. I am writing this book to leave a tangible mark when I'm gone.

Note to Reader

The middle chapters: Buddhas and Bullies, Pinkie, Anything Can Happen in India, and Everything Is Everything and Nothing Is Nothing, are written in the present tense while the rest of the chapters are in the past tense. I decided to just leave them that way, like a crescendo.

Even if you are not inclined to make one of the recipes, please read the sentences under the recipes as they are part of the story.

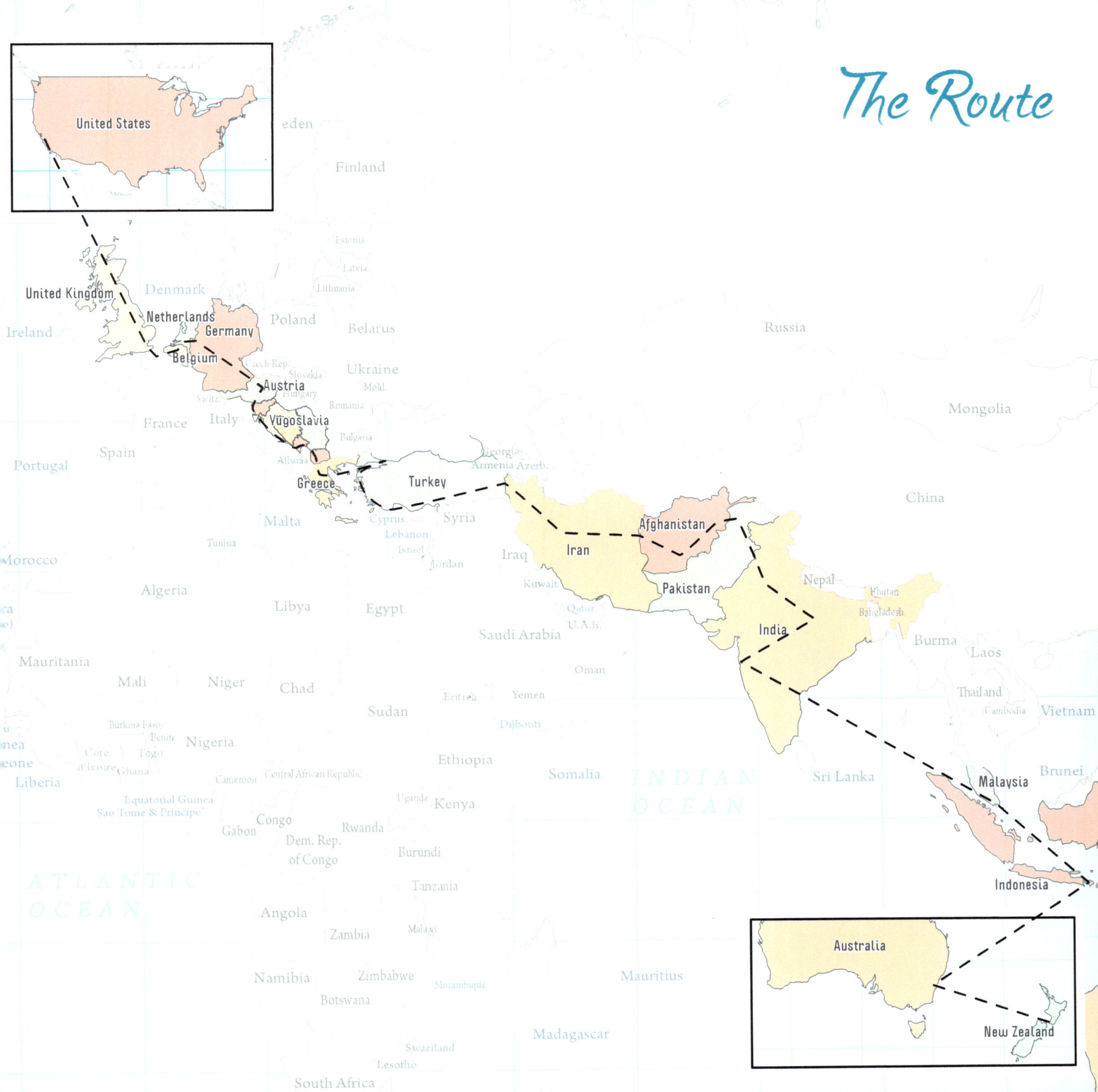

The Route
United States
Canada
United Kingdom
Ireland
Denmark
Netherlands
Belgium
Germany
Poland
Belarus
Czech Rep.
Slovakia
Ukraine
Austria
Hungary
Switz.
Mold.
Romania
France
Italy
Yugoslavia
Bulgaria
Spain
Portugal
Albania
Greece
Turkey
Georgia
Armenia
Azerb.
Malta
Cyprus
Syria
Lebanon
Israel
Jordan
Iraq
Iran
Afghanistan
Pakistan
Kuwait
Qatar
U.A.E.
Saudi Arabia
Oman
Yemen
Nepal
Bhutan
Bangladesh
India
Burma
Laos
Thailand
Cambodia
Vietnam
Sri Lanka
Malaysia
Brunei
Indonesia
Australia
New Zealand
Sweden
Finland
Estonia
Latvia
Lithuania
Russia
Mongolia
China
Tunisia
Morocco
Algeria
Libya
Egypt
Mauritania
Mali
Niger
Chad
Sudan
Eritrea
Djibouti
Burkina Faso
Benin
Nigeria
Cote d'Ivoire
Togo
Ghana
Liberia
Cameroon
Central African Republic
Ethiopia
Somalia
Equatorial Guinea
Sao Tome & Principe
Uganda
Kenya
Gabon
Congo
Rwanda
Dem. Rep. of Congo
Burundi
Tanzania
Angola
Zambia
Malawi
Namibia
Zimbabwe
Mozambique
Botswana
Mauritius
Madagascar
Swaziland
Lesotho
South Africa
INDIAN OCEAN
ATLANTIC OCEAN

Marriage?

Marriage in the hippie era did not get high marks, sex before marriage was "in" and living together was groovy. Commitment was a dirty word and marriage was a state to be feared as it meant being tied down and hitched for life. Chris and I had, at this point (1973), been living together in Carmel Valley, CA for three years.

Chris's parents were divorced and he had fears about marriage. My Jewish parents honored marriage. My living with Chris was very dishonorable in my mother's eyes. My mother called me every Sunday at 10:00 AM and badgered me about getting married. The conversation went something like this:

"Hello."

"Hello, how are you darling?"

"Hi Mom, I'm fine."

"So when are you two getting married?"

"Mom, we've been over this so many times. We both just don't see the point. We're fine the way we are."

"Why buy the cow, if you can get the milk for free?"

"I don't really follow that, Mom. How are you?"

Chris and I talked about marriage and all his fears about divorce came up. Our conversation went something like this:

"Do you think you ever want to get married?" I asked.

"What's the point? Most marriages end in divorce. My parent's divorce was very hard on my whole family, so why bother?"

"Well if we have children, it's better for the children to have two married parents."

"Frank and Sue have little Karina and they seem to be fine."

"You did say you'd consider having children in the future."

"Yes, but we can cross the marriage thing when we decide to have children."

I was disappointed after these conversations but in denial about my disappointment. I wanted to get married and secretly hoped Chris would actually propose, like in the movies. But since I was being bothered by my mother's incessant push towards marriage, I rebelled and said I didn't care. Instead I went to the I Ching (Chinese book of wisdom). I threw the coins and read the passage, which said, "perseverance furthers". I took this to mean "I'll pester him further." I decided to throw the coins a second time. This time I got "cross the great waters". I took this to mean we'll be going on a trip abroad and perhaps to New Zealand where Chris grew up and lived with his family between the ages of ten and twenty-six.

Chris's good friend Nick who had been a boarder at Chris's mum's house in Wellington New Zealand was now living in Berkeley with his girlfriend, Stephanie. Nick and Steph were our best friends and they came to our little rented renovated horse barn where we lived in Carmel Valley about once a month for the weekend. Chris and Nick talked nostalgically about New Zealand and they wove a rosy picture of a place with exotic Maori names and natural beauty. Steph and I became caught up in the dream of moving to New Zealand. Chris represented adventure and a way to get away from my disapproving parents - far, far away.

Chris and I often talked about the possibility of moving to New Zealand. The conversation went something like this: "Do you really want to move to New Zealand?" Chris asked.

"Couldn't we go for a year and see if we liked it?" I responded.

"Well we can't get a visa for a year. They'd probably give us a three month visitor's visa but if we want to stay longer and work, I think we'd have to apply for residency which means emigrating and that would allow us to stay as long as we want."

"If we go for one year," I pointed out, "we may be just getting used to it, but if we go for two years then we'll really be able to see how we'd fit in."

Chris agreed and added, "We won't really be able to decide whether we want to live there, but we need to emigrate to have those options."

"I'll tell my parents it's only for one year, like a sabbatical, because they can relate to that, but I think we should go for two years and really give it a chance and if, after two years, things are not working out, we can come back."

"Sounds good to me," Chris said with a smile on his face. We hugged on it and moved our focus toward New Zealand.

Another underlying reason for wanting to move to New Zealand was political. Nick and Steph and I had worked for the McGovern campaign and when he lost to Nixon in November 1972 we found ourselves saying, "Let's get out of here."

Chris called the New Zealand consulate in San Francisco and they sent us immigration forms to fill out. We decided to drive up to San Francisco to submit our completed forms in person. When we entered the office of Mr. Sharp, the whole environment was distinctly New Zealand. There were enticing ferns with furry brown curly stems planted in pots in the corner of the room. A display of products sold in New Zealand lined one wall: jars of marmite, Steinlager beer, Manuka Honey. Framed pictures of luscious kiwi fruit and tamarillos adorned the walls along with travel posters of glaciers, volcanoes, aquamarine water and pastoral scenes with white fuzzy sheep. I liked every detail of the office. As Mr. Sharp collected our paperwork, we noticed that his glasses were extremely smudged to the point that we couldn't see his eyes through the schmootz. We laughed uproariously for years over that image of Mr. Sharp.

Many weeks later, Chris received a letter from the New Zealand consulate approving his immigration request probably because he had grown up there. However, Immigration denied my application as a single woman teacher, they did not need more teachers. Chris wrote to his mother in New Zealand of the situation and she wrote back with the obvious solution.

"Why don't you get married and Marcia can immigrate as your wife?" It then didn't take too long before Chris agreed that this was indeed the best solution. I don't remember a proposal or an engagement. I just felt very glad that we were finally going to get married.

The following Sunday morning at 10:00 AM the phone rang.

"Hello," I said

"Hello darling."

"Oh hi Mom, guess what?"

"Oh I can't guess, your world is so different from mine."

"We're getting married! We've done our blood tests and we have an appointment with the Justice of the Peace in Pacific Grove next week."

"Oi gevalt, but he's not Jewish."

"Well actually he is a quarter Jewish on his father's side."

"Well how will you raise your children?"

"Neither of us is religious. He won't mind if I sprinkle in a little Hanukah."

"Well I guess I should say congratulations, but don't you want a wedding?"

"No Mom, we just want to get it over with."

"Well can I at least send out announcements to my friends that you have gotten married?"

"Yes, but we don't want any presents as we are trying to get rid of stuff and we want to go live in New Zealand for a year. I can take a one year sabbatical from my teaching job."

We were married at the Pacific Grove Justice of the Peace on June 22, 1973

"Maybe your Dad and I can come visit you in New Zealand."

"Yeah, that would be great."

"Well can we at least throw you a bon voyage party?"

"O.k., but just with the immediate relatives and just before we leave in August."

"Mazel tov, my dear."

"Thanks Mom. I'll talk to you soon."

We were married at the Pacific Grove Justice of the Peace on June 22, 1973. No fanfare for the newlyweds. I was not a glitzy gal. Something simple suited us both. Our friend Sandra was the only witness. Her husband Grover, who worked with Chris surveying, came to the Justice of the Peace on his lunch break and put a "Just Married" sign and some tin cans on our car while we were inside getting married. We drove off to the traditional clang.

My parents were not too disappointed that there was no wedding as my sister had had a nice Jewish wedding in our backyard several years before and it ended in divorce. My mother was just happy that we were married even though Christian Francis Heinegg was not Jewish. They believed me about the one year sabbatical and gave us their blessing.

Chris and I had talked a lot about travel in general and specifically about how we would get to New Zealand and see some of the world along the way. Chris often spoke of his friend, Peter Barrington, who had left New Zealand some years ago with a pack on his back and had gone to Europe and then traveled on the Trans-Siberian Railroad across Russia to Japan and then South through Indonesia and back to New Zealand. Chris was excited about this plan, and it all sounded intriguing and mysterious to me. I had no plan of my own. Chris was four years older than I, had more experience traveling on his own, so I deferred to his travel ability.

We didn't plan the trip from point to point; as Hippies we wanted to be spontaneous. We didn't research the Russian itinerary before we left. We knew only that the Trans-Siberian Railway was the longest continuous rail line on earth covering 6,000 miles from Moscow to Vladivostok and that it was possible to continue by ferry to Niigata on the West coast of Japan. I knew very little about Russia except that Leonid Brezhnev was the head of the Communist Party and I had seen the Bolshoi Ballet in Los Angeles when I was ten. The Cold War was on and I was curious to see just what was behind the Iron Curtain.

We did not collect maps or buy travel guides or phrase books. But we did take a trip to Berkeley to buy Alpenlite backpacks from REI. Chris said that the best down sleeping bags in the world were from New Zealand because of the famous New

Our 'honeymoon': camping at the edge of an English Pop Festival in Kendal, England, August 30, 1973

At Oakland Airport, from left: Chris, Deborah Learner, Louise Taub, Marcia, Peter D'agostino. Raised index fingers signify that this is photo # 1

Zealander, Edmund Hillary, who had climbed to the top of Mt. Everest. Through Chris's New Zealand contacts he bought two Fairy Down sleeping bags that zipped together.

We spent the summer packing our essential possessions into a crate that Chris made for his Honda 350. He planned to ship the crate to New Zealand and we took only the bare necessities in our backpacks. We purchased our American Express traveler's checks with the retirement money I was able to extract from my three years of teaching in the Monterey Unified School district. At this delirious point in our lives, retirement was not a word we understood.

On August 18th 1973, we boarded a British Airlines flight from Oakland, CA to

London as we had decided to go to New Zealand the long way from West to East. And why not? We were young and adventurous. I was nervous and excited to be starting married life on a journey to the unknown.

Postscript: Twenty years later in June of 1993 we held a wedding ceremony to renew our vows in our backyard in Santa Cruz. My parents, sisters and family members attended along with my mother-in-law who was visiting from New Zealand.

Lost in the Mist

When we got to London and inquired at the Russian embassy about taking the Trans-Siberian Railroad, we were told that we'd have to submit our passports; they would be sent to Moscow, and we'd get them back in three weeks telling us whether or not we could go. That sounded way too risky, so we scrapped that plan and decided to hitchhike around England.

Our first hitchhiking experience was a successful one that started just north of London where the Tube ended and the M1 North began. Some bloke picked us up and talked animatedly about England, traffic and specifically how the M1 was more dangerous than the Monte Carlo races due to reckless speeding maniacs. He liked picking up hitchhikers for company and we were headed several hours north with our backpacks for a few days of hiking and hostelling in The Lake district.

After a couple of hours, we pulled off the road and drove into a rest stop. Unlike American rest stops, English ones were large rectangular buildings with an attached petrol station that protected drivers from rain and cold. Their services included a cafeteria, restrooms and a large lounge area with tables and chairs and telephones along the wall.

Although our driver was heading north towards Scotland, he was kind enough to let us off on a rural side road leading off to the lakes; a suitable and safe place to catch the next ride.

No longer than five minutes later, a woman in her forties picked us up driving a Morris Minor and she lived right near the trailhead for the Lake District. Would you believe that she invited us in for tea and scones? And then she took us directly to the "sunset trail", which led over to Lake Coniston where there was a youth hostel we planned to stay at for a few nights.

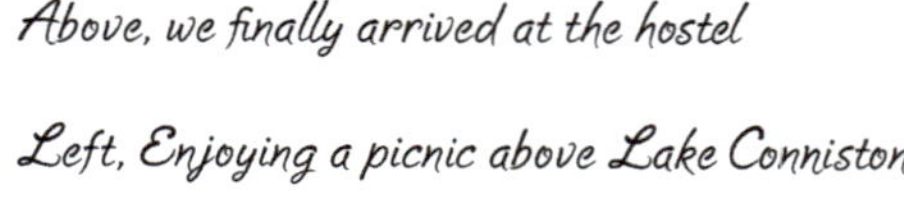

Above, we finally arrived at the hostel

Left, Enjoying a picnic above Lake Conniston

It was about 4:00 PM when we began the hike up the track. We gauged our walking time to be about an hour; plenty of time to get to the hostel before dark. It was a clear lovely day about 68 degrees F. We meandered up the green hills passing heather, brush, sheep, and cows, but no people. On the way up we could see for miles around, but when we reached the top, suddenly a very heavy foggy mist set in. Chris had a map, but due to the dense fog he couldn't find the next trail sign.

After circling around what we thought was the top of the ridge, Chris eventually said, "I think we're lost." I didn't really believe him, because he has a fabulous sense of direction. In the then four years I'd been with him, we had never gotten lost, so I was sure he'd shortly figure out where the path was. He didn't seem at all alarmed and this helped me stay calm. I have absolutely no sense of direction. I'm known to lose my car in a parking lot, or, turn left, coming out of a movie, when others in my company know that the car is parked to the right. I've driven miles out of my way in Los Angeles and San Francisco and gotten lost even with a map. I was completely dependent on Chris's ability to guide us to the hostel.

Chris turned to me smiling and suggested, "Let's take a picture." He set his two inch tripod and camera on a rocky ledge and jumped into the photo." "There", he said, "Now we'll have a picture of us lost in the mist." He obviously viewed this happening as a great adventure.

Not wanting to lose me in the fog, he held my hand as we tentatively walked ten minutes in every direction looking for the signpost to Lake Coniston. Just as Chris began to look really puzzled with eyebrows turning inward, we heard some voices. A few Englishmen who apparently knew the area fortunately appeared and pointed us in the direction to the correct trail down the hillside and into the little town of Lake Coniston.

When we descended, we left the mist behind and arrived in a grassy town square of a tiny village where the sun was out and the people strolled casually in short sleeves. There was a large "safety event" going on with many displays set up by the forest rangers on how to be safe when hiking in this area, or, how not to get lost in the mist. There were tables set up with things trampers needed to be well equipped: flashlights, candles, matches, warm sleeping bags, mirrors to signal for help, water, trail maps and a compass. There were tents set up which had special rain tarps attached and newspaper articles on information boards about what happened to people who were not prepared for the abrupt weather changes on the top of the ridge.

We had every item suggested, except the compass which we promptly bought

Just before the rain came down

and thanked our lucky stars that we were not victims of hypothermia or starvation, which were graphically laid out in a display titled "What can happen to YOU when tramping in this area without the proper knowledge and equipment."

We finally made it to the hostel safe and sound.

Our last hitchhiking experience was on our way back to London when we stood in the rain with our thumbs out for three hours and had our first married fight.

"I'm not hitchhiking anymore!" I cried

"Then, how do you intend to get to the next town?"

"What I mean is that the next hitch will be my last." I stammered.

"Cream-puff, marshmallow." He yelled with his teasing smirk. But he knew he could push me no further.

Soon after a driver finally picked us up but was only able to take us to the next village where I insisted we take a bus back to London.

John's Chips

(Baked potato wedges)

4 large potatoes
olive oil
½ cup flour
1 tsp. salt & pepper
1 tsp. curry powder
1 tsp. mustard powder
1 tsp. chicken stock powder

Scrub but do not peel potatoes. Pre-heat oven to 350° F or 180° C. Put enough oil in baking dish to cover the bottom and place in oven. In a paper bag, place flour, salt & pepper, curry, mustard, and chicken stock powder. Cut potatoes into wedges and shake several at a time in the bag to cover with the dry mix. When all wedges are covered, place carefully in hot baking dish in a single layer. After 25 minutes turn wedges over. Cook for a further 15-20 minutes.

The food in England was lousy especially at the Wimpy Hamburger Bar. The pub food was good; specializing in meat and potatoes. I got this recipe from our English/New Zealand friend, John.

Crossing Borders

The international crowd in the London hostel where we stayed was all going overland to India. We knew nothing about India, but we got caught up in the frenzy of the global flock of backpackers. The Beatles followed the Maharishi to India and since we had no guru of our own, we followed the Beatles along with thousands of others trekking the Hippie Trail, which really started in Istanbul, where East meets West and continued through Turkey, Iran, Afghanistan, and Pakistan to India.

We took a train from London to Dover and a ferry across the English Channel to the continent landing in Calais, France. Then we took a short train ride to Brussels, Belgium where we stayed two nights with my mother's brother, Uncle Bernie and his wife, Aunt Elaine. They were numismatists (coin collectors). From the train station we took a taxi to their apartment that was spacious and full of fine European furniture. Uncle Bernie was to meet us later as he was buying some coins from a Czech dealer. Aunt Elaine, who was from Missouri, took us out to dinner at a fine French restaurant. When she ordered for us in French with her Southern accent I was most amused.

The next day, Uncle Bernie drove us around Brussels' main square, the Grand Place, in the rain showing us the ornate buildings and then to a numismatist convention. In a large hall, long tables were set up and everyone was milling around buying, selling and trading coins. Many numismatists bought for investment. My Aunt and Uncle actually made their livelihood with coins. Others were there as hobbyists. Some collected coins with favorite animals and others with pictures of famous people in history. I was fascinated as I already had a small stash of coins from different countries back home in my parents' attic.

Our brief visit ended with a tearful good-bye at the train station where we choo chooed off to Amsterdam, a likely place where Hippie travelers were to be found.

In the Amsterdam hostel where we were staying, we saw a notice on the bulletin board that read: "Have van - looking for others to travel to India - share petrol. Leave a message here if you're interested. Brian."

We met Brian Livingstone in a smoky Amsterdam pub. He was a hip English/Jewish legal aid lawyer with clean wispy black shoulder length hair and intense eyes hiding an impish sense of humor. I thought he was appealing; Chris thought he was intelligent and we both got on well with him, sipping our beers and talking about the planned trip to India.

Brian picked up a red pen and we followed his squiggly line across the map of Europe. He said, "I've been to Europe several times and I'd like to pass through Germany, Austria, Yugoslavia and Greece fairly quickly and then slow down when we get to Istanbul where the real journey begins."

Chris responded, "That's fine with me as I spent two years traveling and working in Europe a few years ago."

I piped in, "I spent my third year abroad in Italy and France, but we'd like to stop in Vienna and visit an aunt of Chris. My mother was born in Vienna, but she was brought to the U.S. as an infant."

Chris added, "My parents lived in Vienna in their early adult years."

Brian asked, "How long would you want to spend in Vienna?"

Chris said, "A night or two would be sufficient."

Brian agreed as his pen moved along the map from the known to the unknown and ended in Istanbul. We agreed we'd go slower in Turkey, Iran, Afghanistan, and Pakistan and arrive in India around Nov. 1st. We clinked our glasses to seal the deal and sang out "Cheers."

Changing the subject, Brian queried while scrunching up his nose, "I don't suppose you are fans of your president Richard Nixon?"

I responded, "No way, I worked for George McGovern and when he lost, we figured it was time to leave the country."

Chris added, "We're actually going to go live in New Zealand, where I grew up but we wanted to go the long way through India."

The next day we were off in Brian's green VW camper van, listening to tapes and singing along to the Beatles, the Rolling Stones, Jefferson Airplane and Eric Clapton, etc. That afternoon we approached the German border with trepidation. Brian said nervously, "I don't think the German border guards are going to be kind to us long hairs."

"Especially us Jewish long hairs," I added.

Brian replied, "Maybe Chris should drive, he looks Aryan."

Chris answered," I'm actually one quarter Jewish and it's a bit too late now," as we were already only one car away from the border kiosk. Chris continued, "You're driving a Volkswagen, they'll like that."

"Passports," demanded the German border guard in a gruff voice. We handed our pass-

XNF 611L

ports to him. He looked at them and then back at us and said. “Pull your van over there for inspection and everyone out.”

As Brian pulled the van into the designated parking place, he said, “See, I knew this was going to happen.”

Chris said ‘We don’t have any dope, so there is nothing to worry about.”

Brian replied anxiously, “You know they’ve been known to plant stuff on hippies.” Beads of sweat appeared on his brow as we stepped out of the van. We were instructed to sit three feet apart on a bench and not to talk to each other.

My thoughts/prayers ran on and on something like this:

”Oh God in Heaven, please let them look through the van, find nothing suspicious and let us go.”

“Could Brian be right - they plant some large quantity of heroin and we’re imprisoned? I’ll be sent to a Women’s prison separated from Chris and Brian.”

“Anne Frank, Nazis, Gestapo...SS...”

“My poor great Aunt Molly, what camp did she die in? Was it Theresienstadt or Auschwitz? And Chris’s Uncle Otto? I think he died in Auschwitz and he was brought up Catholic though he had a Jewish name: Feichenfeld (means violet fields.) Will they know that Brian’s family changed their name from Leibowitz to Livingstone?”

I squirmed, bit my lips and had to go to the bathroom, but my thoughts continued to torment me.

“They won’t kill us for smuggling dope, but it could be a long time in prison. Do the Germans honor the one phone call? My parents won’t be happy about this.”

“Brian is a lawyer - maybe he’ll have connections.”

Only a half hour went by and they told us to get back in the van, gave us our passports and the all-clear move-on signal with the wave of his German gloved hand. We sighed with deep relief as we drove quickly through Germany.

Throughout the trip in the VW, I remember sleeping out in our sleeping bags just off the road on fine nights and cramming into the van in inclement weather. We bought food and made our rice and veggie meals on our little Primus stoves on the side of the road.

We stopped for one night in Vienna where Chris and I stayed with Chris’s stout, matronly, spinster Aunt Evi who lived in an apartment with large pieces of early 19th C Biedermeier furniture. She actually looked a little like her furniture with her square torso, but she was welcoming and we enjoyed a shower and a good night’s sleep in a real bed with an eiderdown. The following day she took us out to lunch

where we ate bloodwurst - a sausage patty made of cow's blood. The entrée was Wiener Schnitzel, Austria's signature dish.

A few days later we were basking in the sun on the coast of Yugoslavia near a town called Split, where we swam off the rocks of the Adriatic.

Several days later the three of us drove further East to Skopje. In the marketplace Brian and I bargained for apples, oranges, potatoes, peppers and eggplant with traveler's sign language and smiles. I had a delightful feeling that I was then really in the midst of a very different culture; one I knew little about. Although we were in Yugoslavia, it felt Russian to me as the women were dressed in their traditional clothing that resembled those Russian dolls that all stack inside one another.

Tooling along, we picked up Jon the Greek who had been backpacking around Europe for three months and was on his way home. He was the epitome of Zorba - lively, cheerful and fun. Brian had been very apprehensive at border crossings with his long hair, but Jon pacified his fears by telling him he was friends with the guards at the Greek border.

Our VW approached the Greek border and Jon salivated as he saw his friend, the border guard. Pointing wildly he said, "There's Stenos." Before the van came to a complete stop, Jon jumped out and ran over to Stenos and we watched as Jon hugged Stenos with a chest thump, a full-arms-around-each other-hug and several slaps on the back in addition to kisses on both cheeks and then another round of chest thumps and a look into each other's eyes. They were obviously good friends who hadn't seen each other for a long time, or was this just the way Greeks greeted one another?

They jabbered away in Greek for ten minutes, and then Jon dragged Stenos over to our van and introduced us. Stenos spoke a leetle English. He said, "Jon's friends, my friends, you come, I give you special Greek stamps, passports please."

We handed him our passports and he took them into the border booth and returned them to us with two colorful Greek stamps. Meanwhile Jon hugged several other border guards and Brian, Chris and I looked on in wonder.

Brian said, "This is fuckin' beautiful."

I said, "What a major contrast to the German border."

Chris said, "The Germans could learn a few tricks from the Greeks."

Jon jumped back into the van and we all waved enthusiastically to Stenos with a chorus of "epharisto" (thank you in Greek).

Just before getting onto the motorway from the border compound, Jon spotted these two gorgeous young women hitchhiking. He said, "Ooo la la," as he licked his lips.

Brian said, "I want the brunette, you can have the blonde."

"Can we pick them up?" Jon asked turning to us with pleading eyes. "It's only about an hour to my mother's house where we can all stay. Brian pulled the van over as Chris and I nodded that it was o.k. with us.

Wendy and Susan climbed in and Jon engaged them in conversation about himself and his three months traveling in Europe and about where they had been and where they were going. Now we were a congenial group of three men and three women. Brian hooked up with the Canadian from Winnipeg and Jon with the American from New Jersey.

We pulled up to Jon's mother's house, which was adjacent to his family's resort right on the beach just outside of Thessalonica. His mother came scurrying out with her arms stretched forward. She wore a pink sweater under her floral mid-calf cotton dress and a full apron over it. Her gray hair showed briefly under a headscarf tied in back under her bun. She looked warm and round, like my Sephardic grandmother although she was probably only forty-five years old. We were surprised that she greeted us as if we were all her long lost children, hugging each one of us. She fed us and gave each couple a little cabana on the beach.

Romance flourished for one week as we swam and lounged around applying sun

Sunbathing on the coast of Yugoslavia

Jon the Greek gives a welcoming wave

tan lotion on each other's backs and chatted together about our travels. We walked a short distance up to the town for breakfasts and in the evening for dinners at the Taverna. The excellent Greek food, of which Moussaka was our favorite along with the Greek wines, retsina and ouzo mixed with the Greek dancing created an intoxicating experience. We celebrated my twenty-ninth birthday singing in Greek and clapping and watching a Greek man do the traditional dance with a bottle on his head while standing one legged on the top of a small round table.

The next day while we were recovering from our hangovers, lying on the beach, Chris and I overheard the following conversation between Brian and Wendy:

"I really want you to come to India with me. It will be so great to experience India together." Brian whispered.

In surprise Wendy responded, "But I've only just met you and although I want to spend more time with you, I really only want to travel in Europe."

"India will open your mind to the spiritual and because it is supposed to be such a mind-boggling place, we will have a bonding experience which can last a lifetime."

"How about we go to Crete for a week together and if we're still close, I'll go to India with you." She suggested.

"Great, I'll do it." I'll just have to tell Chris and Marcia of my change of plans.

Brian took Chris and me aside the evening before we had all planned to leave and told us regretfully that he could not continue with us to India, that he wanted to pursue his relationship with Wendy on the Island of Crete. He offered to drive us to the Thessalonica train station the following morning where we could catch the Oriental Express to Istanbul. We agreed, as we supported him in his decision, and wished him luck although we were disappointed, as we had traveled so cooperatively together.

The next morning, in Brian's stupor of love, he backed the van into Jon's mother's clothesline full of wet clothes and knocked it down. He was very sorry and extremely embarrassed but she was not at all upset, as she had enjoyed the week with the youthful group filling her house with laughter.

Postscript: We heard through the grapevine several months later that Brian and his girlfriend made it to India together, but then broke up in Bombay.

Wiener Schnitzel

2 pieces of veal	oil to deep fry
½ tsp. salt & pepper	1 lemon
flour or breadcrumbs	parsley
1 egg	cranberry sauce (optional)

With a meat mallet (available in any kitchen store) tenderize meat by pounding it into ¼ inch slices. Season meat with salt and pepper to taste. Prepare 3 plates. Put flour in one, beaten egg in another and breadcrumbs in the third. Then dip meat slices in plates in order mentioned. Put oil in frying pan ½ inch deep. Get the oil hot enough that the schnitzel sizzles immediately when you put it in. When it has the desired color, turn it over. Schnitzel fries at high temperature in 2-3 minutes. Squeeze lemon on top and serve with parsley sprigs on the side. Cranberry sauce or apple sauce go well with schnitzel.

I included this recipe because it is the specialty dish of Austria and a favorite of the Heinegg family. I usually make it for Chris on his birthday.

Moussaka

1 eggplant
1 lb. ground beef
1 onion
¼ cup olive oil
4 large tomatoes
½ cup flour
1 egg
½ cup milk
cheese
salt & pepper

2 cups Bechamel sauce:
2 tbsp. butter or olive oil
1 ¼ cups milk
2 tbsp. flour
salt & pepper

Melt the butter in a sauce pan. Stir in the flour and make a smooth paste. Heat the milk and pour into pan continuing to stir as the sauce thickens. Add salt and pepper to taste. Lower the heat and cook 2-3 minutes while stirring.

Cut the eggplant into ½ inch slices. Salt them and set aside. Chop the onion and sauté in oil. Add the ground beef and sauté til cooked. Plunge the tomatoes into boiling water until the peeling comes away from the fruit, then remove with a slotted spoon to cool on a plate. Peel the tomatoes and then mash them with a potato masher and add them to the meat mixture. Add salt and pepper to taste. You may want to add some water to make it saucy. Simmer on low.

Prepare the dough: In a flat bowl, put a ½ cup flour, 1 beaten egg, ½ cup milk, 1 tbs. oil and mix. Pour oil into a frying pan and heat. Then dip each slice of eggplant into the dough and fry until brown. Grease a large baking pan and make layers with eggplant, fresh thinly sliced cheese (goat, cheddar or jack) and meat mixture. Cover the whole thing with béchamel sauce and bake at 350° for 45 minutes.

This is our favorite Greek recipe. It takes a long time to make, but it's worth it!

The Pudding Shop

From London to Amsterdam to Vienna to Thessalonica, we had heard over and over through the backpacker's grapevine: "You must go to the Pudding Shop when you get to Istanbul." Turkey is the crossroads where East meets West, where Europe meets Asia and Istanbul is its capitol. It used to be called Constantinople. In fact, Turkey is the only country in the world that has land on two continents.

Upon arrival in Istanbul, in October 1973, we went straight to the Pudding Shop eager to see what everyone was raving about. The Pudding Shop was in the old section of Istanbul called Sultanahmet, named after the Sultan Ahmet. It was located on Divan Yolu Street, opposite the Blue Mosque, one of the most prominent landmarks of Istanbul with its blue dome and six minarets (spires).

Idris Colpan and his brother Namik opened Lale Pastahanesi (The Pudding Shop) in 1957. At that time, it was the only place in the area where the adventurous tourist could get information on Turkey and direct transport to Asia. The tourists made The Pudding Shop famous, using it as a meeting place and message center. Local people came in and out, mostly workers, but the customers were travelers on the Istanbul - Katmandu Hippie Trail. Parked across the street from the shop were VW vans and old beat up cars of every variety. The restaurant had six tables on an outside patio under an aluminum awning. Inside there were a dozen rectangular tables where different groups of people ate and shared stories. The whole main wall was a bulletin board where scraps of paper with messages and information were tacked up for the tourists.

The place was crowded when we entered. We met people in The Pudding Shop who had traveled to India and were now returning through Istanbul and were passing on very important information on transport, accommodations, restaurants and exciting things to do and see. There was no *Lonely Planet* Turkey when we were

Human mules on cobblestone street in Istanbul

traveling in 1973, so this oral information was most useful. We were warned of pitfalls and ways to conduct ourselves at the borders. For example, getting a haircut was a good idea for longhaired males and wearing a headscarf and a long skirt was appropriate dress for women. The cardinal rule for those on the overland to India trail was to not carry any marijuana across a border, as you might end up in jail. But there was plenty to be had within each country.

The Pudding Shop served a creamy milk and rice pudding called *sütlac* along with other tasty, filling and cheap food. All the restaurants in Turkey had open kitchens for the tourists. Rather than being seated, offered a menu and selecting what you'd like, we were guided into the kitchen where we could smell the wonderful aromas of spicy beef and lamb stews, fritadas, okra in an aromatic tomato sauce and rosemary scented shish-kebabs. We were asked to just point and a server would put a plentiful portion on our plate. The food was superb!

For me, the food was just like my Sephardic paternal grandmother used to make. My grandparents were born and raised in Turkey and immigrated to Los Angeles in 1907. For a few years my family lived in my grandmother's house after my grandfather had passed away. Although I was only four years old, I remember helping my grandma cook Sephardic food which is a mixture of Greek, Turkish and Spanish cuisine: kalamata olives, feta cheese, dolmas (rice wrapped in grape leaves with lemon) and green beans stewed with tomatoes and onions. Our family's specialty dish was fritada (a quiche of spinach, cheese and eggs).

One of the most striking images in the cobbled stone streets of old Istanbul was of a man carrying a refrigerator on his back and others carrying wooden and cardboard boxes tied onto a square pillow to cushion the load on the carrier's back.

Other images were of 1960's large American cars mingling with goats, carts filled with vegetables and goat's horns pulled by horses, and men screeching around on bicycles and motorcycles. Cans and paper littered the streets while smiling schoolboys in navy blue smock uniforms with white collars scampered around and dodged men in child's pose who were praying to Allah.

Men smoking elaborate water pipes and dropping squares of sugar into their tiny teacups were commonplace both on the sidewalk and in the bazaar, which was an amazing giant market place spread through miles of city streets under canvas coverings. Everything was sold including piles of goats' heads, brightly colored handmade rugs, jewelry with exotic stones and beads, embroidered blouses, fragrant and unusual spices, hardware, sheets, and books in many languages. The place had a musty dusty hashish smell. I heard the clang of pots and pans and hookahs being

bought and bargained for as we wandered through this unusual area.

The golden nugget of tourist information we gleaned at the Pudding Shop was that you could get a student ticket on a cruise ship in the Istanbul Harbor tourist office and sail around the coast of Turkey all the way to Iskenderun in East Turkey. For the incredibly low fare of $8.00 you could sleep dormitory style in the depths of the ship for eight nights. We jumped on it and bought tickets using our phony student cards, which we had purchased in London through the student underground network. I joined four other girls in the dormitory and Chris met the partners of these girls in the men's dormitory along with a few cockroaches. We student ticket holders were not allowed on the upper decks where the German tourists dined and sunned themselves on the striped lounge chairs.

No food was included in our student fare, but the ship stopped at noon each day at seaside resort towns with lots of open kitchen restaurants. We five couples would march into a restaurant and eat enormous amounts of mouth watering Turkish food. We would pack up the extra food we couldn't stuff into our tummies and kept it to eat for dinner on the bow of the ship as the sun set. Before we left the little towns we also purchased fresh bread and fruit for breakfast for the next day. Was this heaven or what?

Fritada De Espinaca

(Spinach Souffle)

- 2 packages frozen chopped spinach
- ¾ cup grated parmesan & romano cheese
- 2 tbsp. matzoh meal or breadcrumbs
- 2 eggs
- 2 tbsp. olive oil

Thaw the spinach. Place spinach in mixing bowl, do not drain. Add beaten eggs, oil, matzoh meal and cheese. Mix well and pour into greased baking dish. Bake uncovered at 350° for 45 minutes.

I got this recipe from my mother, Taube Caraco, who adapted it from her mother-in-law, Mathilda Caraco , Brusa Turkey. I adapted it slightly. It is our family favorite and made for every pot-luck.

Mystery on the Oriental Express

On the eighth day our Turkish Cruise ship pulled into the Port of Iskenderun, in South Eastern Turkey on the Mediterranean Sea bordering Syria. Our group of ten Western trekkers disembarked, as we were all heading northeast towards Iran while the real cruise ship passengers would be returning to Istanbul. Since other backpackers going through to India from Istanbul took a train straight through Turkey, we were an oddity to the locals in Iskenderun.

We asked a few curious men how to get to Lake Van in the north where the Oriental Express train heading east would stop. The people were very friendly and each person we asked wanted to personally escort us to the bus station. We eventually rode in a Dolmush (Turkish Taxi) to the station, boarded the bus and in a few hours were at Lake Van purchasing tickets for the overnight train to Teheran.

At 6:00 PM we boarded the train headed toward the Iranian border. The seats in our train coach faced forward in pairs, like on a bus. I had expected a compartment with long seats facing each other and a sliding door opening out to the train hallway like in European trains I had seen in the movies. There may have been a dining car and compartments and sleeper coaches somewhere else on the train, but we were relegated to the lower price coaches. Other passengers on our section of the train were Turkish and Iranian men dressed in sports jackets.

A train conductor dressed in a formal uniform with brass buttons came around and collected our tickets and passports. We assumed he was going to take them into his "office carriage," stamp them and return them to us. The office carriage was a little train room with a curtain instead of a sliding door, making it look like a mysterious Kasbah. A few hours later, our passports had not yet been returned and we were getting nervous.

Suzanne, one member of our traveling group, wondered, " What's taking them

so long to return our passports?"

"They are probably making plans as to what to do with us," responded her boyfriend, Bill.

A few of the guys went looking for that conductor, but couldn't find him anywhere. At 9:00 PM when it was dark outside, the train stopped suddenly in the middle of nowhere, an empty platform in the desert. We were told by the conductor to get off the train and that another Express train would come pick us up and take us east; the train we were on was headed south on another track. We refused to get off without our passports. The conductor was adamant that we get off this train because that other train would pick us up and he indicated our passports would be returned.

When we bought the tickets, we were told it was a non-stop trip to Teheran. All of us were quite confused, scared and angry so we all got off thinking it was better to stick together.

The "so called" train depot where we waited had no conveniences: no toilets,

coke machines, telephones, no information booth, nothing but some benches. We always carried snack food with us, but we didn't know how long it would be before the train would arrive. It was cold, 45° F, but we were dressed warmly. It was a clear night; the stars were out but it was spooky and we imagined the worst plots taking place.

Marilyn was really worried and said, "I can't believe this! It's so confusing! Could they send us to prison?"

Carol added to her fears by firmly stating, "I'm really scared they have evil plans for us. We could be tortured or hung, although we haven't done anything wrong. If we get out of here alive, we'll go to the American Embassy in Teheran and tell them how we've been treated."

Then Tom put fear into all of us with his vision when he announced, "They will probably send the women to a whorehouse and the men to hard labor. Hey, any of you read *Murder on the Orient Express* by Agatha Christie?"

Bill said, "Yeah, that was the best of Agatha Christie's mysteries. The murder was so well thought out by the nine people who stabbed that swine."

Carol interrupted, "This is not a murder, just a mystery."

My mouth was dry like an old cracked volleyball. I didn't know what to think; the atmosphere was tense, but I couldn't imagine heinous cruelty. I thought Carol and Suzanne were exaggerating the situation but I knew Tom was putting us on.

Chris interjected. "The train we're going on is not the Oriental Express which is referred to as the Orient Express in that murder story."

I piped up, "It's not! Oh, I'm so disappointed! I thought we were traveling on that famous mysterious train."

Chris explained. "We're riding on the Ottoman Railways. The original Orient Express went from Paris to Vienna. Later the route was extended to Istanbul, but it never went through Turkey to Iran. The Orient Express was a luxury train patronized by royalty, nobles, diplomats, and businessmen – the bourgeoisie in general, not the likes of us."

Chris whispered his apprehensiveness to me, but refrained from contributing to the scary scenarios of the others. "According to the American Embassy tourist info, one should never surrender one's passport. And here we are in the middle of nowhere stranded. I don't think there is another town anywhere nearby. It's so unnerving."

Tom tried talking to some Turkish men who had also gotten off when we did about our passport situation but the language barrier was stiff. We overheard a man saying, "Train, train" with his arms waving this way and that. I thought he was reassuring us that a train would come. Tom pointed to his watch, but the man shrugged his shoulders indicating that he didn't know when it would come.

It got colder and the wind came up. We couples alternately huddled together on the benches and took walks up and down the platform to keep warm.

Finally, at midnight, we heard the snorts of a train in the distance. We perked up and gathered our packs. When the train came to a full stop, a conductor got off and commanded us to board quickly saying, "Teheran, Teheran."

Our guys said, "Passports, passports." The conductor just kept pushing us on to the train. The train chugged on a few miles and a different conductor appeared at the front of the coach and formally announced, "Passports" with a stack in his hand. He then called out each person's name having difficulty with pronunciation. When my name was called I walked down the train aisle towards the conductor and accepted my passport feeling like it was a diploma at my graduation.

Buddhas and Bullies

It's October 26th 1973. The Van Gouloo Express train from Teheran has come to the end of the line at a very small station in the middle of nowhere but close to the Afghani border. Chris and I and the four other western couples we met on the cruise ship are on a bus crossing the border into Afghanistan from Iran.

The atmosphere at the Afghani border is a carnival. Handmade drums and flutes are playing; hippies and Afghanis are dancing in the sunshine. It's an all-afternoon party reminiscent of many we've been to in Golden Gate Park. It is a completely different atmosphere than in Iran, which is dark and frowning and oppressive. What is the lightness in these people? They seemed to enjoy the hippie flow of westerners eager to play with them. Is everyone stoned? The cardinal rule on the Hippie Trail is DON'T CARRY DOPE OVER A BORDER. Yet, joints are passed in restaurants. Does this make sense? No, that is what is so notable about the EAST; nothing makes sense to the western mind.

All the bus passengers must go from the passport/visa stamping booth to the health verification station to the currency declaration post and finish up with the customs search. We are of course, clean.

In the late afternoon, after the festivities, we all get on another bus for a two-hour ride to the small town of Herat. Chris and I are seated in the back row of a short squat school bus. I am sitting next to two Afghani guys in their twenties. We introduce ourselves easily. Abderachim and Gulhamad are lively and laughing types. They want to engage and I am delighted to get to know some Afghanis. They teach me words in Pashtó: Pochánseh - thank you, chirta dah - where is? posáday - How much? They know a leetle English. We pantomime and I point to his turban.

"How do you say "turban" in Pashtó?" I repeat the word and they laugh their

heads off, obviously at my pronunciation. Their laugh is so infectious that I am laughing and laughing, too.

Abderachim puts his turban on Chris and asks, "Your uncle?" Then he roars with laughter. Their smiles are sweet and open. We bump along the paved but desolate road, nothing to look at but some mountains in the distance and dusty brownness.

Somewhere along the way the bus stops at a roadside restaurant, which is more of a hut. It has a bathroom! All the passengers disembark for fifteen minutes. I go into the "ladies room" which is your basic hole in the concrete, with two women dressed in burqa, the Afghani women's dress. Before entering the stalls, the two women fling off their burqas and to my surprise underneath they are wearing purple pedal pushers from the fifties and chartreuse cotton blouses! The women are in their twenties and giggling in Farsi. I am shocked by the loud colors and amazed by their youth. My imagination pictures older women in traditional dress. I'm thinking how limited their vision is through the small 3x5 screen they must look through. I'm curious but too shy to talk to them. I accept that this is the way it is. Afghani women are not seen in public without their burqas, but hang them up when they come into their houses.

We get back on the bus and arrive three hours later in the small town of Herat. Afghani "tour guides" approach us smiling and saying, "Hotel, *baksheesh.* I take you to hotel, *baksheesh."* We learn quickly that *baksheesh* means money. It means: " I'll take you to a hotel, and you give me a tip *(baksheesh)*. It means, "I won't do anything, just give me some money." The traveling rule is: if you give to one, you have to give to everyone, or be bombarded. But one is bombarded anyway with the screech of *"baksheesh."* I am told to develop an invisible shield to just go about your business and they'd leave you alone.

There is no need for a guide as the town consists of a few streets and only one hotel. The shops are like cubbyholes with wooden doors that open out to the street. Naan bread is in one shop giving off that wonderful "fresh bread smell". Another shop is selling lamb meat ridden with flies. Another sells backpacks left behind by travelers or traded for other goods. REI and Northface from Berkeley are the most popular.

We are very tired but the excitement of our first Afghani town is intoxicating. We all come to the grand Hotel Paradees. We check in and go to our room passing other trekker friends in the hallway that we have met previously on the Hippie Trail. We hug each other and exchange pertinent travel information, like, "Hey man, where've ya been?"

The room is clean with two single metal frame twin beds with thin kapok mattresses and nothing else. I mean nothing: no pictures on the wall, no dresser or nightstand, only one naked light bulb in the middle of the ceiling. I go down the hall to the bathroom, which is a hole in the concrete. It is so smelly and filthy I gag and feel sick and I cry. I am weary from travel and feel I'm just not tough enough. I keep wondering; is this what it is going to be like all the way to India?

After a rest, we head downstairs for the evening meal. The restaurant in the hotel is warm with a long rectangular low table and cushions all around the perimeter of the room. We are seated and the manager passes joints around to relax his guests. We decide whether we want lamb or vegetarian. The main meal is usually lamb couscous

and vegetables with a yogurt cucumber salad. The food is yummy if you can get over the image of the flies on the meat in the market place.

After the main course, we are presented with a five-item dessert menu in English, all of which sound scrumptious. By this time, we are all so stoned that we are drooling over the sweets. The most popular dish is a crêpe with apples and a carmel sauce with vanilla ice cream and pomegranate seeds sprinkled on top. You can order as many desserts as you like and Chris eats four crêpes. The dinner lasts all evening until most of us have fallen asleep slumped over on each other in a stupor - quite the den of iniquity!

On our first full morning in the town of Herat, we wake up late and discover it is the beginning of Ramadan and there is a carnival in the streets; we are feeling very fortunate to be here during this time. Ramadan falls in the ninth month of the Islamic lunar calendar, and is a month of blessing marked by prayer, fasting and charity.

The men of the town have spent weeks building a ferris wheel completely out of wood. We marvel at the work involved as the dads spin the ferris wheel by hand. The children, both boys and girls, laugh as their fathers crank the ferris wheel. There are a few women around hidden in their burqas, but we see mostly men and children at the carnival. Women are at home preparing the evening meal to break the Fast of Ramadan.

Although it is 1973 and I have ridden a steel ferris wheel run by electricity at the Santa Monica Pier, it feels like we have now gone back in time to the middle ages. A wooden handmade and hand cranked ferris wheel? In fact, when we entered the Hippie Trail, at the trailhead in Istanbul, it was a little like going through the wardrobe doors into Narnia: ancient languages, unfamiliar customs and dress.

Several days later we enter the capitol of Afghanistan, the grand city of Kabul. We stay at the Green Hotel, which is characterized by a giant chess set in the outdoor tiled courtyard. The larger chess pieces are two feet tall and the pawns are one foot. The players actively pick up each piece and place it in a new square as other hotel residents look on from their balcony rooms. I am fascinated. My maternal grandfather taught me how to play chess when I was twelve years old and I plot better moves in my head than the players I am watching.

Meanwhile Chris has been getting information on which side trip to take: a trip to Bamiyan to see the great Buddhas or a longer trip to Mazar-I- Sharif known for its famous Blue Mosques.

We review the information together and decide to go to Bamiyan, a mountain village above Kabul. But first we must get our visa extended one week. Franz, a fellow traveler from Berlin says, "It's a simple procedure, go to za police station, fill out za form and they'll grant you an extension. No problem."

The next day the police station is closed for some unknown reason so we wander the streets of Kabul where half the people are dressed in what looks like beige pajamas and the other half are in suits and ties and carrying briefcases. I am most surprised to find some working women in mini skirts and heels carrying briefcases while other women are dressed in the traditional burqa.

We attempt again the next day to do business at the police station. As we enter, we see a jail cell on the right with a disheveled Spaniard yelling "van a matarme." "They are going to kill me," I translate to myself slowly; my intermediate level Spanish comes in handy here and I ask him why he thinks they are going to kill him. He replies that he has been caught with an expired visa. I digest this information in my little brain, but my gut tells me that they are not going to kill him - perhaps detain him. I try to reassure him that he won't be killed. The police seem pleased that I've calmed him down. But what do I know about Afghani criminal law? We are a bit shaken, but we proceed to the next window, submit our form and get a one-week extension to make the side trip to Bamiyan. We are warned that we must be out of the country by the stamped date.

We set our mental alarm clock for 5:00 AM in order to meet the Russian open-backed jeep at 6:00 AM for the trip to Bamiyan. There are twelve of us, mostly Afghani men, a few boys, and a variety of goods. After traveling two hours up a mountain road, we stop at a small village and Chris buys an apple turnover from a bakery stand. We bump along for the next six hours trying to keep the dust out of our throats by wrapping a shirt over our mouths, but I see Chris's eyes and read his body language. He is in excruciating pain from GAS and the evil apple turnover. His New Zealand machismo holds out with his stiff upper lip but not a peep of complaint comes out of his mouth or anywhere else.

At last we arrive as the sun sets in this small mountain village. Bamiyan was the Buddhist Center in the First Century. Generations of Buddhists built the immense Buddhas over a one hundred year period.

We're ushered into a restaurant/hotel, which is one large room with a pot-bellied stove in the middle surrounded by thick carpet. This is where, for the next few days, we sleep in our sleeping bags, eat and tell stories, and listen to Afghani sitar playing. It is freezing outside but toasty and cozy inside.

Some warmth is felt by noon the next morning and a small gang of boys take us through some caves at the foot of the Buddhas.

We join a group to climb a winding narrow staircase carved into the limestone mountain that encases the Buddha. On a platform at the top of the Buddha's head, we spend three hours meditating. I have never meditated before but I am awed into silence and peacefulness sitting high near the forehead above the third eye on this magnificent statue. I am very near to God, and the dust and ruggedness of the trip so far fades away into the distance. I don't really want to come down but the tour guide says we must descend, as the gates will be closing for the night.

At dinner, we hear that there is a possibility that we can purchase tickets on a private plane back to Kabul for $25 each rather than taking the Russian jeep. An Indian Film Company charters this plane for their actors as a movie is being made on the outskirts of Bamiyan. We go to the movie-filming site in order to purchase the tickets. The scene of the movie that is being filmed repeatedly is of a jeep being blown up and the actors being thrown out of the jeep with Indian ketchup spurting about. We watch this over and over eleven times. Chris is fascinated but I've had enough after a few takes.

The really big event of the weekend, The *bouskatchi,* the National Afghan game, is about to begin. We trek to the other side of town following the crowds attending the big game - Bamiyan against Mazar-I- Sharif. On the way we see a brightly colored truck with at least fifty people jammed together on the top careening down the road between the white birch trees and watch little girls picking up dry dung to take to their mothers to burn which keeps their houses warm.

We finally come to a natural stadium - the valley below with the dusty brown dirt hills surrounding it. People are pouring in and sitting on their haunches. Vendors are selling watermelon slices to the crowds as they wait for the event to begin. The two teams of horsemen are lined up facing one another with the goat head ceremoniously placed in a ring between them. The ram's horn is blown and the teams charge each other. Each horseman tries to scoop up the dead goat's head and gallop as fast as possible to the goal posts on either end of the playing field. We scream and yell and root for Bamiyan while slurping watermelon along with the rest of the crowd. Not being a sports fan at all in the States, I amaze myself with my own enthusiasm. Bamiyan wins and the crowds go wild, yelling and throwing watermelon rinds in the air. I don't really know what the score is.

As soon as the game is over we scurry over to yet a third part of town where the chartered plane is about to take off for Kabul. Feeling already exhilarated by being on the winning team, we board the twelve-seater plane for the fifteen-minute flight to Kabul with two famous Bolllywood actresses dressed in elaborate saris and

bangles. We are dressed in the same thing we've been wearing for months, tee shirts and jeans, lumbering along with our backpacks. In Kabul we land and walk down the steps of the little plane directly behind the actresses. A crowd of fans, clapping excitedly greets us. I wave with a big smile on my face pretending to be an actress that is part of this entourage.

Back in central Kabul, we spend one more crashed out, stoned night at the Green Hotel and board the bus the following morning for the daylong trip over the Khyber Pass into Pakistan. We wind our way up and up a treacherous one- lane dirt road spiraling endlessly up and around in a nauseating sequence of twists and turns and stomach hollowing glances down the cliff side of the road. The road is so

Bollywood actress leaving Bamiyan

narrow that I can't see the road from the bus window, only the valley thousands of feet below. I think about the traders who came through this pass throughout history with their silks and spices, and about the famous Ghenghis Khan and the humble ordinary Abdul.

At the very top of the Khyber Pass and about a half an hour from the Pakistani border we stop and a Pakistani official comes on board to check passports. All the passports are handed forward and looked over. Then names are called out and recipients struggle up to the head of the bus to retrieve their passports. Our names are called out in perfect English. "Christian and Marcia Heinegg must go back to Kabul." We have no exit stamp on our passports! Evidently we were supposed to have gone back to the police station before leaving Kabul and gotten an exit stamp on our one-week extension visa, which we did not know.

We look out the window of the bus and see that our backpacks have been taken down from the top of the bus and are being transported to a waiting area to return to Kabul. Chris frantically argues with the bus driver and the Pakistani official. I can see things are not going well and I am very worried. My stomach is in knots. I hear everybody screeching, "baksheesh" and I conclude that we need to bribe a few people and save ourselves the windy trip back to Kabul. But my self-proclaimed tight-ass husband is not easy about offering bribes. While he tries to haggle the bribe down to something he considers fair, I cry loud and billowy tears. The bus driver takes pity on me and a price is agreed upon. Next stop: Pakistan.

Postscript: March 12th 2001. Chris and I are sitting in our living room of our Santa Cruz Gardens home and we are watching the Buddhas that we had been to in Bamiyan being blown up by the Taliban on CNN. We are crying and outraged. How could they do this?

Aush

½ cup yellow split peas
1 cup kidney beans
1 bunch spinach
1 onion
1 lb. ground lamb
I package fettucine
salt & pepper to taste
½ cup tomato puree
1 ½ cups plain yogurt
3 tsp. mint
½ tsp. hot chili pepper flakes
¼ cup cilantro
oil for frying

Wash split peas and put in saucepan with 1 ½ cups cold water. Bring to a boil then cook on low for 40 minutes until soft. When cooked add kidney beans and keep warm. Wash and chop spinach and steam. Saute onion in oil and then add ground lamb and brown. Add tomato puree and salt and pepper to taste. Mix mint, chili, cilantro and more salt & pepper to taste with the yogurt. Cook fettucine according to directions on package. Mix together meat mixture with spinach and yogurt mixture and serve over noodles.

This is a an Afghani stew and it is delicious! I remember eating this in the Afghani restaurants and I wrote down the ingredients in my trip diary. The only difference is that they made their noodles from scratch.

Pinkie

The bus that took us over the Khyber Pass from Afghanistan into Pakistan, has brought us to the city of Lahore. I don't like Lahore, mostly, because of the name. Our hotel is a seedy one where we befriend, or are befriended by, a traveler named Pinkie. We spend only two nights there passing through to our real destination, India.

Pinkie is an Englishman, with a big E, about our age. He has traveled several times overland from England to India. He is about 5'9", thin of stature with dusty brown lifeless hair. He wears light trousers and a muslin sports jacket. Pinkie, which is of course his nickname, is well dressed unlike the other hippie travelers who wear jeans and wrinkled shirts. He is a character out of a movie of colonial India. He imagines himself to be a Raja. Pinkie tells us that his greatest dream is to command a large entourage of tourists assisted by Indian servants carrying umbrellas to protect the group from the heat. In his dream, he sits elevated on one of those Indian platforms with fringe hanging all around and is carried by four Indians. Elephants carry the luggage of the touring group.

Upon leaving our hotel rooms throughout our trip, we have used a secret way of tying our packs, invented by Chris who is a New Zealand Boy Scout expert in knot tying. After a brief walk to the main square of Lahore we return to our hotel for a rest and find that our packs are broken into, as they are retied differently. Yes, one pair of cuff links I bought as a present for my father is missing. Chris tells Pinkie about it and Pinkie immediately takes it upon himself to remedy the situation.

He says, "I know how to handle these Pakistani Hotel managers".

At first the hotel manager says, "It couldn't be any of my staff" and tried to brush him off. I wasn't there to witness Pinkie's finesse, but before we left, the cuff links were returned.

The next day we are walking with Pinkie who wants to change money. But he doesn't do it like the other travelers who would either go up to a teller at a bank or make a money exchange with a black market exchanger. No, Pinkie goes into the bank with us in tow and asks to see the manager for some "important business". He is ushered to a desk and he orders, almost demands, a cup of tea. We are included in this order for a cup of tea. He conducts his ordinary business of cashing some travelers checks with a flurry of gestures a Hollywood movie director might make.

By now we are "traveling friends" of Pinkie so we decide the following day to share a cab from the Lahore Hotel to the border between Pakistan and India. Here again Pinkie's arrogant stylized personality emerges along with his obsession with ordering cups of tea in the oddest places. The cab driver stops at a gas station. We are in the back seat and Pinkie is up in front with the cab driver.

A young Indian boy, perhaps nine years old walks by us with a circular tray balanced expertly on his left shoulder with three cups of tea and three cream-filled buns. He is headed from the restaurant where he works across the street to some customers in an office building. Pinkie summons him like a dog, "here boy". The boy approaches the cab and Pinkie reaches out the window and passes us each a cup of tea and a cream bun. He pays the boy an appropriate price and a good tip. But now the boy has to go back to the restaurant and get another round of tea and buns for the customers that ordered them. We are aghast, but somehow taken in by his peculiar charisma.

It is at the border that he tells us to go ahead of him as he has some business to attend to that he wouldn't want us to be involved in. We then become suspicious.

I ask Chris, "What do you think of Pinkie?"

"He's mysterious and intriguing and I'm fascinated by his demeanor."

"He made me feel uncomfortable when he ordered that boy around like he was a king." I countered.

"Yeah, but he was so well mannered and debonair about it."

"I'm not sure I trust him. He seems so cool, calm and collected but there is something shifty about him."

Chris was quiet for a moment, and then said, "Some might label him a con man, maybe justifiably, but I like him and trust him because he's been helpful to us."

We enter India, the final destination of the overland to India journey. In my mind the drums are playing and the cymbals are crashing. In reality it's a quiet walk about a block long on a dirt road (the no-man's land between these two often warring countries). Every twelve feet, there is an Indian official sitting cross-legged on a small rug with a typewriter. We stop at each station and another form is filled out each with different information. We collect maybe ten pieces of paper with our names and one other item of information like where we came from, the amount of money we are carrying, how long we're planning to stay, etc. I am thinking this is the most bureaucratic border, but look how many people they are employing with something important to do. And in the distance, *I see elephants!!* We are indeed in India. We have arrived. Pinkie finally emerges on the Indian side of the border and he is visibly sweating from fear.

We stay at the same hotel with him that night in Amritsah and he tells us his inspection experience with the glee of success as his plan worked. Evidently, Pinkie is smuggling a baretta, a small old English pistol in his pants under his belt. He is planning to make a profit selling it on the black market which he has done successfully a few times before. He distracted the border officers by declaring less money than he actually had. He wanted them to suspect something fishy and thereby take attention away from the gun. Then he admitted his mistake about the amount of money he is carrying and was allowed to enter India.

Tomorrow, Pinkie is off to do his business on the black market and we are headed to New Delhi. We never asked him what his real name was. He was just Pinkie.

Anything Can Happen in India

The Taj Express train travels from New Delhi to Agra in two hours. It is mid-November, mild winter in the northern part of India; slightly cool nights and mornings and warm in the afternoons. We sit across from an Indian man whose head is hidden by his newspaper. In big letters, the headline reads "FLU HITS DELHI."

Immediately, we feel feverish and headachy, whereas just ten minutes earlier we were healthy. Suddenly, I have a sore throat. We look at each other with the same surprised expression on our faces.

Chris says feebly, "Can the power of suggestion bring on the flu symptoms?

I say, "Anything can happen in India." I reach into my pack for a few Vitamin C.

The train whizzes along. The cows, giraffes and elephants seen through the train windows blur passed us. I regret that we are on an express train, as Indian country life goes by in fast forward. My head feels like it is filled with asbestos.

We arrive in Agra, site of the Taj Mahal, one of the eight wonders of the world.

Abruptly, fear grips Chris in his debilitated state and he says, "The rickshaw drivers will rip us off and I'm too weak and confused to bargain."

I reassure him, "We'll make it through, we'll find a place to stay and rest."

Chris is pale, he coughs, holds his stomach and with great effort puts his pack on and gets off the train. We smell the curried samosas sold on the train platform. If Chris had been well, he would have run to catch up with a samosa vendor and bought a few of his favorite snack. But today the smell nauseates him.

The rickshaw drivers swarm around us ringing their bicycle bells. God is good, and we are rescued by a soft-spoken rickshaw driver who is atypically tall, with very dark brown skin, a black bushy mustache, and beard which wraps from ear to ear. He wears an orange muslin turban wrapped around his head, which means he's a Sikh. His eyes are a milky blue

CHANNEL
MITSUMI TUNNER JAPAN
AVAILABLE IN 5 MODELS

grey and in them I see a compassionate soul.

He seems accustomed to sick western travelers and says, with sincerity in his voice, "I will take you to a very nice place where they will take good care of you."

Our usual suspicion of rickshaw drivers weakens and we climb into Latif's shiny red and black rickshaw. It is a long ride into the countryside outside of the city of Agra. We are too pre-occupied with bodily pain to take in our surroundings. The hurriedness and the harassment of beggars and trinket salesmen fade as Latif cycles away from downtown Agra. We are feeling more peaceful and Latif's manner is kind.

Twenty minutes later, he rides into the grounds of a complex of bungalows operated by the Indian government for tourists. It is simple, low priced, clean accommodations. Our room has two single beds, a nightstand in the middle and our *own* bathroom. The room is stark, no framed pictures on the walls.

Latif says, "Pop into bed and my friend Satish will bring you some medicine." We do as we are told. Sure enough, a short elderly Indian man wearing typical white muslin pajamas shuffles in to meet us and brings us our medicine consisting of a cup of chai and buttered toast with fresh garlic slices spread liberally on top. This is all we eat for three days.

Satish says, " Sip, eat my garlic toast and sleep and you will be well in three days." We follow his instructions to a T; we sleep and anticipate the footsteps of Satish and the smell of the garlic. We are too feverish to read, write or talk. Since garlic is an antibiotic and it is offered with reverence we become believers. True to his word we are in three days miraculously cured.

I say to Chris, "I am utterly amazed at the power of garlic".

Chris says, "Anything can happen in India."

I ask, "Do you think we can get enlightened here?"

Chris responds, "Maybe, though I don't know exactly what that means."

Latif returns and says, "I see you are now beautifully fit and ready to see my Taj Mahal."

Postscript: Over the past thirty-five years, Chris and I eat garlic toast when we feel feverish.

Samosas

4 medium potatoes	1 medium onion
½ cup frozen green peas	1 tbsp. olive oil
½ green chili	½ tsp. ginger
½ tsp. garam masala	2 tsp. curry powder
1 tbsp. cilantro	salt to taste
cashews & raisins (optional)	chutney
1 15 oz. package refrigerated pie crust	

Peel, boil and mash the potatoes. Chop and sauté the onion. Thaw green peas. Finely chop the green chili and the cilantro. Grate the ginger. Measure the garam masala and the curry powder and mix all ingredients with the potatoes. Add salt. Add a few chopped cashews and raisins if you like. Roll out prepared refrigerator dough. Cut out 4-5 inch circles (a small plate can be used to cut around). Cut circles in half. Take one semi-circle of dough and fold it like a cone. Place a spoonful of the potato filling in the cone and press to seal the opening. For authentic samosas deep fry until golden brown. Another method is to bake them on a greased cookie sheet in a 375 oven for 25 minutes. Serve with chutney.

We love samosas! This recipe is authentic except for the packaged refrigerator pie crust. I tried the bake method which tasted great but the samosas were nothing like the ones we had in India.

Everything Is Everything and Nothing Is Nothing

Searching for enlightenment is the goal of many of my fellow travelers going overland to India on the Hippie trail. Chris and I, however, are just out for adventure. We are in the dark about enlightenment.

"What is it?" I keep wondering. Some people are going to an ashram in the North and others to that one in the South. They are following Guru Whoozit and Baba Gobbledegook. I haven't a clue as to what this enlightenment and guru business is all about. My religious repertoire includes Judaism, Christmas and Easter, no Buddhist, Hindu or other spiritual realms.

"Enlightenment, does it mean to see the light?" I ask myself.

"Yes, the light of God" whispers a voice in my head. Being a good student, I search for and find an English dictionary and look up "enlightenment."

Definition #1: "enlightenment is the state of being enlightened, informed as an enlightened populace that is free from prejudice and ignorance." I don't know where there is a populace like this. It must be referring to utopia.

Definition #2: (Buddhist) "the state of heightened perception in which the individual transcends the mind and body and attains Nirvana." Oh dear, now I have to look up 'Nirvana'. I remember back to the late '60s when I lived with my cousin Louise Taub in the Bernal Heights area of San Francisco and our phone number actually spelled Nirvana and we thought that was so cool. The dictionary indicates that Nirvana is the Buddhist idea of heavenly peace; the condition in which the soul is free from all desire and pain; perfect happiness reached by the complete absorption of oneself into the supreme universal spirit. I can only relate to this state of mind by recalling my various acid trips.

I contemplate these new mind-blowing ideas and find myself thinking, "It's a lot to absorb." I am twenty-nine years old and I am not "on a spiritual path to enlightenment." I wake up each morning in my "Marcia Way," putting one foot in front of the other. I see the good in people and I'm excited about fulfilling my dreams. But I am curious about the concept of enlightenment.

It's November 1973. While we are in India, we are going to see my cousin Jack, who is a follower of Meher Baba. Jack is 5' 8", slim, a bit wiry, and strong. He is four years older than I am - the same age as Chris. He is a very funny man. Jack went to Reed College in Portland, Oregon, a highly academic offbeat college. He was a Biology major and his mother, my Aunt Dora, hoped he would become a doctor so she could say to her friends, "My son the doctor." After college, Jack joined the Peace Corps and lived in Ethiopia for two years. It was a very meaningful part of his life. He taught science there and absorbed the Ethiopian culture. When he returned to the USA he lived on the East coast for three years and trained Peace Corps volunteers going to Ethiopia.

After the Peace Corps Teacher Training adventure he moved to the Bay Area and felt he was at a crossroads in his life, which eventually led him to living in India.

The compound where Jack lives is in the small town of Ahmednagar, East of Bombay, six long bumpy hours on a bus. When we get off the bus, we follow Jack's detailed directions and we walk across the street to the entrance of the compound.

As we enter the main gate, an Indian man, fifty years of age, with a warm welcoming demeanor, wearing glasses and dressed in western clothing (white short sleeve shirt, khaki muslin pants) greets us and says, " I am Adi."

I respond, "I am Jack Caraco's cousin Marcia and this is my husband, Chris."

Chris says jokingly, "Is this where we will get enlightened?"

Adi replies, "Everything is everything, and nothing is nothing". We are not at all sure what he means but he also tells us where we can find Jack, who at that point is walking up and greets us. Adi is the CEO of the Meher Baba Community and Jack is his Administrative Assistant.

We walk to Jack's rectangular 20 x 40 foot cement bungalow and find that he has set up a white muslin mosquito proof tent especially for our privacy in the middle of the room. We settle in a bit and begin to make dinner with Jack.

Chris asks, "Well, if everything is everything and nothing is nothing, what are we going to have for dinner? Everything or nothing?"

Jack replies, imitating the Indian accent and shaking his head, "Meher Baba tells us that we need to look at the other side of the coin - that everything is not black or white."

I inquire, "You mean, read between the lines?"

Jack affirms, "Acha" meaning 'you got it'. Jack and I can't stop imitating the Indian accent and shaking our heads but Chris does not join us in this ridiculous practice.

Chris asserts, " If everything is everything, and nothing is nothing, then everything is nothing, and nothing is everything."

Jack says "acha". We laugh and continue to chop onions and garlic, mix in chopped carrots and spinach and stir it all into the sizzling pan with curry and chilies.

As we are preparing the meal, Jack tries to interpret Baba's philosophy to us, every new thought opening up more questions.

Chris asks Jack, "Is Meher Baba your Guru?"

Jack explains, "Yes, in a way, because a Guru is basically a wise man, a Spiritual Teacher. But Baba is an Avatar."

I'm confused and ask, "What's an Avatar?"

Jack expounds, "An Avatar is the embodiment of God. You see, God came into the body of Meher Baba just like He previously came into the bodies of Jesus, Mohammad and Moses."

Chris interrupts our serious dialogue, "Do you have any peanut butter?" All this talking and shaking our heads and chopping are making the wait for dinner a long one and Chris is a hungry peanut butter fiend. Jack passes Chris a bag of peanuts in their shells and a mortar and pestle with some instructions as to how to make peanut butter Indian style.

I ask Jack, "Do you believe in reincarnation?"

"Yes, we believe we keep coming back in a new body to learn. We do learn from our mistakes and our experiences. We are reincarnated many times until we reach Enlightenment, and then we stay with God."

I remind Jack, "Jewish people don't believe in reincarnation."

Jack answers saying, "I know, that's why it's hard to talk to my mother. She thinks I'm crazy."

I am suddenly delighted with the whole idea of reincarnation. For me it's very positive. Instead of just dying dead and being gone forever, I will come back and live several more lives as I have a lot to learn.

I announce, "In my next life, I want to be a very tall, strong male person and I want to surf." Jack and Chris laugh at me and we finally sit down to eat dinner.

Rented bicycles are our means of transportation around Ahmednagar, which everyone calls "Nagar." On a Sunday we ride out to the house where Baba's closest disciples live. It is the house where Baba lived with his partner, Mehera. It is called *Meherazad*. There is another place on the other side of Nagar called *Meherabad,* which is where Meher Baba's body is buried. I keep getting the *Meherabad* and the *Meherazad* mixed up.

Chris shares an easy way to remember the difference between *Meherabad* and

Meherazad. "Remember that *Meherabad* is the place where Baba's body is buried because of the many "bs" in bad, Baba, body and buried."

Jack says, "In Sanskrit, 'bad' means to flourish, while 'zad' means free. At *Meherazad,* where everyone goes on Sundays to feel more free, to relax, hang out, and eat, the Mandali (disciples) tell stories of traveling with Baba all over India and America."

As we bicycle to *Meherazad* that Sunday morning we pass a group of women at a well. I'm in rural India and I feel like I've arrived. They are filling their shiny brass pots with water. A few are leaving with pots on their heads. I notice a circular piece of twisted cloth on their heads used to balance the heavy pots of water. They are wearing rural everyday work saris. The colors are drab grey, brown, olive green and dirt rose.

A young girl with one black braid stares at me with her hand on her hip and her elbow pointing directly at me with an interested yet stern look on her face. I am curious about her too.

It seems like we are the only ones traveling on this five-mile stretch, as it is very peaceful, although we do occasionally see a few locals on bicycles, motorcycles, a few bullock carts, and a truck or two. We pass one brick house set back from an acre of corn and another with an aluminum roof.

We see a woman squatting on the ground by the side of the road, sorting the corn kernels in a rectangular pan and discarding the bad ones. She is wearing a dark green sari with a gold colored blouse. She has the red dot on her forehead and a very large gold ring in her nose with colored bangles on her wrist.

We pass another group of women repairing their mud house. One woman is on a ladder slapping wet mud on the walls and smoothing it out with her hand. Another woman below her holds a metal pan of wet mud on her head from which the other women scoop the mud.

While bicycling down the dusty road I ask Jack, "How did you come to Baba?'

Jack replies, "Well, when I came to the Bay Area after my Peace Corps life, I was

facing the "Who Am I " question. It was 1968 and everyone was finding themselves through marijuana, acid and mushrooms. So I joined right in. I was reading Aldus Huxley and Carlos Castaneda and tripping out. I was staying with Leon (our common cousin) in a pad in San Francisco when someone gave me a business card with the phrase "Don't Worry, Be Happy" on one side of the card and a picture of Baba's heart-warming, laughing smile on the other side with the words, "I love you more than you'll ever know. I am God in human form." I tucked this card into a special pocket in my Ethiopian vest."

Jack continues his story. "The drugs in San Francisco were messing with my head so I decided to go back to Boston where I started listening to tapes by Baba Ram Dass. On one of the tapes it was revealed: "Meher Baba is your real guru, as he is God in human form." Jack added, "I also heard from somebody at Sufi Dancing that in January 1969 Meher Baba had dropped his body, which meant he died, and that his body was buried and enshrined in a special place called Meherabad, in India. I then met a woman who carried Baba's picture, and a man who had actually met Baba. While this man was telling me of his own experience of meeting Baba, I saw Baba's laughing eyes through his eyes. Then I knew I was meant to visit the Meher Baba community in Myrtle Beach, South Carolina. There I became hooked on Baba and after that, Baba called me to India."

While bicycling back to Jack's compound later that Sunday I remark to Chris and Jack, "Meher Baba's phrase, 'Don't worry, Be Happy' sounds so simplistic, but everything we've learned in our three weeks here is most profound." We finally figured out that everything is everything and its opposite, nothing is nothing, means you can't figure things out - so stop trying and enjoy life.

Jack points excitedly to the sky and says, "Look at Baba's beautiful painting." We look up and see incredible splashes of red, yellow, orange and purple in the amazing Indian sunset. We are starting to see the light in our awakening enlightenment.

Postscript: Jack becomes an acupuncturist. His mother is able to finally say to her friends, "My son the doctor." My spirituality starts to blossom as a direct result of my Indian experience with Jack and his clear interpretation of Meher Baba's teachings.

Bamboozled in Bombay

It was December of 1973 when we were bamboozled in Bombay by a black marketeer and the Bank of America. A conspiracy of 'B' words. Though the "black market" was illegal, we trekkers changed money on it as it was the thing to do and one got a better exchange rate. We lived frugally and wanted our travel budget to last, which meant that every rupee counted. The reason it was called the black market was because business was often done at night - in the dark and out of sight of the law.

We had exchanged money on the black market several times in India. A guy would approach us and say out of the side of his mouth, "You want to change money? I give you good rate." Then his eyes would look left and right to indicate that we should go into some back alley or restaurant where we could do our dirty business either in private or in the anonymity of a cafe.

That day in the park, we did our black market exchange in broad daylight. It was only in the twitching of our bodies and shifting of eyes that one could tell something was illegal. We were walking across a small city park around noon on a sunny day, when this Bombay trickster, whom I'll call Mr. Bull Shit Artist, approached. He was 5'9", wore western clothing, had a mocha chocolate handsome face with black-coifed hair. He looked to me like the Indian movie star from "Bobby", the musical costume-changing extravaganza we had just seen at the downtown movie theater. We were on a grassy hilltop and there were no people in our immediate vicinity when he said, " Do you want to change money?"

We carried our money in American Express traveler's checks. We wanted to change $400, which was in four checks. Mr. BSA said, "Look, I'll take the checks into that bank across the street and I can assure you that I will get you the very best rate of exchange because I know the bank manager." Chris and I glanced at one another to figure out if we wanted to give our checks to this guy. I usually deferred to Chris who later told me that as long as we didn't counter sign the checks, it would be o.k. We then gave him our checks in a mesmerized stupor. Mr. BSA continued with his instructions, "You wait here and I'll be back in ten minutes."

At that point, we realized that we had lost our minds completely. Our brains slipped down our shirts and down our jeaned pant legs and spilled out on the streets of Bombay.

Mr. BSA walked off with our traveler's checks leaving us still in the bubble of believing he'd return with our money. We moved closer and watched him go into the bank. We saw through the big bank windows that he didn't speak to anyone in the bank and then we saw him go out a different door and disappear into the crowd on the other side of the building. We ran after him. First we ran towards the bank but realized it was not a bank at all, but a police station. We madly ran after him around the building and into the crowd on the other side but we had lost him. We already felt like criminals and therefore couldn't go into the police station to report him. We pushed our way through the crowd of Bombay urbanites for a block or two before we gave up.

We were in a state of shock, then Remorse, Guilt and Blame set in. We had just lost most of our remaining money. I had a sinking feeling in the pit of my stomach. Nothing had ever happened like this, as we were usually so careful. It was such a beautiful day and we were relaxed, perhaps a bit tired and caught with our guard down. It was as if a spell was cast. Remorse stabbed me with his knife in my stomach causing tears to well up in my eyes. Guilt engulfed me in a grey layer of culpability. Blame shoved us toward each other accusingly. We headed back to the park with our heads hung forward and down dejectedly.

"How could we be so fucking stupid?" Chris shrieked. I didn't have an answer.

We circled back and reached the park and sat down on the grass and I asked in a panicky voice, "What should we do now?"

"We'll have to go to the American Express office and they will probably replace our checks."

I felt my stomach lurch knowing I would have to lie. It was a warm sunny day and as I looked across the park I saw two women in their colorful saris walking with their toddlers. It was a normal day for them, I thought. "What will we say as to how we "lost" our checks?" I puzzled to Chris.

"We'll tell them we were pick-pocketed on the train. It happens all the time. Do you have your copy of the traveler's check numbers?"

"Yes", I squeaked, "I'm sure they're tucked away in the super secret compartment of this pack." I produced them easily and Chris found his too.

"Now we just need to find the American Express office." Chris concluded.

Two crowded bus trips later; we walked into the American Express office trembling.

Chris approached a general information window with me shrinking by his side and announced coolly, "We've lost our traveler's checks." The man barely glanced at us, looking up briefly from his paper work. He handed Chris some forms to fill out. We went over to a table with four chairs like in a library and I filled out the forms with Chris whispering our lie to me as I wrote in our answers to the questions: when, where and how did you lose your traveler's checks, and their worth?

We took the forms back to the window and turned them in. The man skimmed them and said, "You can pick up your re-issued checks tomorrow after 9:00 AM"

That was it, it was that simple! The next day, we picked up our checks with no problem and went to the cemetery to bury Remorse, Guilt and Blame and the memory of Mr. BSA. We walked amongst the gravestones and tried to pronounce the Indian names, and that helped us get a grip.

Next in the conspiratorial B category was the Bank of America. We needed more money from our account in Carmel Valley, CA to purchase air tickets from Bombay to Singapore to Bali to Sydney to New Zealand, our final destination.

Chris has a superlative sense of direction and ability to locate places on maps and find the specific transportation needed to get anywhere in the world. A few hours later, we were in front of the tall modern Bank of America buildings.

A vast impoverished shantytown circled the many storied, wealthy financial buildings. The shacks, which served as houses, were made of whatever could be found: bits of aluminum, wire fencing, latticed woven palm leaves, blankets and clothing. They could hardly be called houses or tents, perhaps hovels. It was hard to imagine people could live in these conditions, yet they were living and dying before our very eyes. The children were barefoot walking through debris. Yet they smiled at us and seemed happy to have their picture taken. No lawn chairs in front of shantytown, the adults sat on their haunches on the concrete and talked among themselves as their children played with found objects; tires, sticks and stones.

We went into the spotless bank which inside looked like any branch of the Bank of America in California. We went up to the teller and said that we wanted to have money wired to us from our CA branch. The man said that he could arrange that, no problem. We showed him our bankcards and he filled out some forms and said, "Since today is Friday, and Monday is a bank holiday, your money will be available on Tuesday next week."

We thought this might be the case and had already decided to spend the weekend in the state of Goa, an overnight boat ride South of Bombay.

But before leaving the Bank of America, Chris said, "Let's take the elevator to

BANK
AMERICA

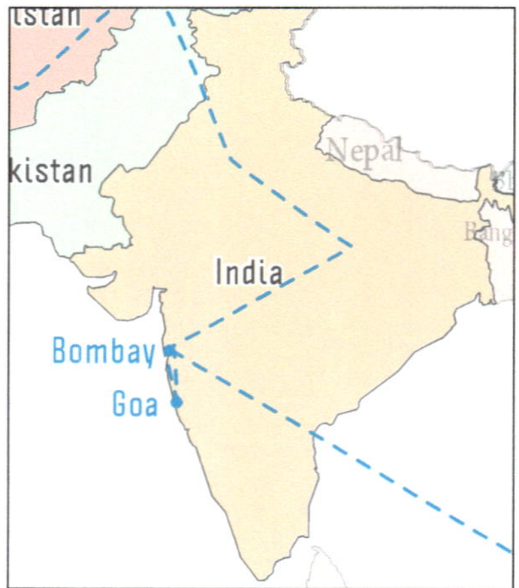

the top floor to see the view." Happy to be finished with money business, I quickly agreed. Chris snapped several pictures from this high vantage point.

The very wide gap between rich and poor was so clear from above, and from the twentieth story one could see all of sprawling Bombay.

That evening we caught the ferry to Goa. At sunset the ferry sailed away from Bombay and it felt like a San Francisco ferry to Angel Island. We slept on the deck on long benches. The next morning we arrived in Vasco Da Gama, the largest city in the smallest state of India; the size of Rhode Island. Portuguese merchants first landed in Goa in the 15th century and annexed it soon after. The Portuguese colony existed for about 450 years until it was taken over by India in 1961.

Goa was tropical with swaying palm trees right on the beach. We stayed in a thatched hut a quarter of a block from the calm lapping shore of the Indian Ocean. We ate chorizo and felt like we had been transported to Mexico. I met a goat that I named Paco. Chris loved watching the fishermen go out in their dugout boats.

We felt more relaxed when we returned to Bombay three days later. We entered the Bank of America at 9:00 AM on Tuesday, and Mr. Gimi, the teller, said, "Sorry, your money has not arrived - check back tomorrow." This was not at all surprising as things didn't work to schedule in India and we knew from Meher Baba that patience was one of life's lessons. Not wanting to take out our frustration on kind faced, no problem, Mr. Gimi we walked out and roamed the streets of Bombay.

Just up from the Bank was the pharmacy. The red turbaned man and his son were enjoying their chat as Chris snapped their picture. Laid out on the ground were bottles of varying herbs, seeds, tinctures, nuts and other unknown bits of digestibles seemingly for one's health. There were also animal skins and a couple of small taxidermied animals.

Next we stopped at the seller of "beeties". Here crushed beetle nuts were wrapped in leaves and smoked cigarette style. We smoked beeties earlier in India and since we were smokers in those days, we treated ourselves to a beetie. Many Indians chewed the beetle nut and spit out its red insides, which looked like a glob of blood

when it landed on the street.

Having just written a letter home, I waited in line at the post office behind a white cow. Then headed towards the edge of town to have a chat with the camels. Chris tried to hitch a ride, but the camels were not in the mood.

Wednesday morning we headed back to the bank, a ten-minute walk from our hotel. The streets were empty of taxis, cars, buses and motorcycles. Men and boys were playing soccer in the streets. We asked someone about what was going on and were told that there was a major transportation strike. We'd never seen anything like it in India. We asked someone else if the banks were closed and he said, "Yes, everything closed," as he kicked the ball and ran.

Thursday morning, our third try at getting our wired money from the Bank of America was "bingo" day, thus ending the conspiracy of 'B" words. We bombed out of Bombay leaving the smarmy black marketeer and the Bank of America behind.

Swiss Air Flight # 777

The dense chaos that is India receded into the distance and for some eight hours we were suspended in "Switzerland" – a neutral place. Our Swiss Air flight from Bombay to Singapore was like swirling in warm chocolate and rolling over into fluffy eiderdowns.

I experienced on-board comfort in their meal of Wiener Schnitzel, mashed potatoes, green beans in butter, and a glass of Riesling with a piece of Swiss cheese and apple for dessert along with a chocolate truffle.

As he gazed out of the window, Chris was giddy with the seeming lightness of our plane gliding through the blue sky amidst white puffy clouds. He enjoyed the window seat so much when we flew that I let him have it as I enjoyed watching him marveling at the aerial view and pointing out sights below that he recognized. "Look there's the Bank of America building, bye bye."

I thought, "What a boy Chris is; he likes airplanes, boats, cars, and motorcycles. Various vehicles must have been his favorite toys as a child. He's told me many times about the model airplanes he built as a teen that are stored in his mother's attic. I'm looking forward to seeing them when we get to Wellington."

Chris smiled broadly at the neat and shiny airhostess who asked him what he wanted to drink, and he said, "something sparkly please". Pushing the button to the relaxed back position, he said to me "I feel so taken care of."

"Me too," I agreed opening my mixed nuts and savoring my favorites, the cashews.

Chris continued, "I'm so relieved to be away from the beggars and hawkers in Bombay."

"Yeah, and the poverty and seeing so many people with deformities," I added. "Yet the peacefulness in the countryside seemed spiritually serene compared to the city."

"I didn't know how much I missed western comforts." Chris responded as he licked his lips after the last bite of truffle. " Have you had enough curry?"

"No," I replied, " I absolutely love Indian food; I'd like to try making samosas."

Chris remarked, "Oh there are lots of Indian people in Wellington, I'm sure we can get good Indian food there."

"Oh good," I said, "I wonder what the food will be like in Singapore?"

The Singapore spread

A Fishy Story

The Singapore night market was about two blocks long. Rectangular tables were set up side-by-side, each with round outdoor table umbrellas and lights hanging under plastic lampshades. The vendors chatted with their spouses and children and paid little attention to the customers except when you wanted to buy or taste something. Their transistor radios played Chinese music low in the background.

I mostly remember fruit and a vast array of fish laid out on the tables. Papaya, oranges, watermelon, honeydew, custard apples, plums and a few unfamiliar fruits were sliced and ready to eat and whole fruits were on the tables ready to buy and take home. It was the same with the fish; some raw and sliced ready to eat with a toothpick and some whole fish laid out on ice for purchase. There were some pig feet hanging and other prepared foods like fish balls for tasting. The dominant smell was fishy, but fresh.

The rhambutan and the dukhi fruit were strange to me. Seeing the red hairy round fruit the size of a plum intrigued me. I was offered a slice and I'd say its taste was a cross between plum and watermelon. The dukhi fruit were as big as cantaloupe with spiney protrusions like porcupines and they made me scrunch up my nose as they stank like rotten eggs. Although, I was curious, the smell repelled me and I didn't try it.

On the third night of our one-week stay in Singapore, the cleanest city in the world, we were seated at a small round wrought iron table for two at an outdoor café. It was Dec. 29th, 1973 and the evening was balmy, 78° F. We wanted to avoid other tourists and high prices, so we asked our hotel manager for a "worker's restaurant" and he recommended one only a few blocks away.

Our table was outside exactly at the corner of a busy intersection. Cars, mo-

Singapore night market

Hairy, red rhambutans and spiky, smelly dukhi fruit

torcycles and bicycles whizzed around the corner. We could have high five'd the bicyclists as they passed.

Our waiter brought us a menu completely in Chinese. Chris pointed first at the waiter and then waved his hand over the menu. I put my fingers in my mouth hoping that the waiter would understand that we wanted him to choose for us and just bring us a meal. He got it without more pantomime.

First came an aromatic bowl of fish soup. The broth smelled very fresh and tasted delicious, simply prepared with a few pieces of white fish, carrots, celery and bok choy. Next he brought two small bowls of rice and two oval shaped dishes of mixed vegetables: carrots, celery, water chestnuts, broccoli, green beans and bok choy; all recognizable.

Then came bowl after bowl of shellfish. I recognized lobster; crab, clams, mussels, shrimp and squid, but there were several more crustaceans on our table that were species unfamiliar to us.

Along with the shellfish came various utensils used to pull out the meat; tiny forks, tweezers, pliers and a few peculiar wrenches.

Chris and I pulled and tugged and cracked and slurped for a while and then I looked up and because the shells were piled up so high on the table, I couldn't see

Chris. I asked, "Are you there"?

"Yeah, I'm here, isn't this fun? "Slurp slurp," Where are you?" I looked to one side and Chris leaned to the other side and then we switched and burst out laughing at the ridiculously high pile the shells had made. Our laughing shook the table and some of the shells fell to the ground. Fortunately, our waiter came to our aid and took away some of the plates full of empty shells.

He then brought us a small menu, which we assumed was a dessert menu. We were too full and waved it away and made a scribbling motion to indicate we were ready for the bill which came to a grand total of $5.00 U.S. for two. With heavy bellies, we strolled down the street and back toward the night market and Chris said, "I wonder how high their cakes might have been stacked?"

Singaporean Scallops

1 lb. bay scallops	½ tsp. salt
1/2 jar Peanut Satay sauce	½ tsp. sugar
1 package noodles	1 tsp. oil

Wash the scallops and cook them in oil for 5 minutes. Add Peanut Satay sauce and stir in salt and sugar. Serve over noodles cooked to package directions with any steamed vegetables.

I looked up Singaporean recipes and the first one I found was for Fish Head Soup which I didn't think I could handle. This second recipe is the easiest recipe I've ever made!

Trapped in Paradise

We flew from Singapore into Denpasar, the biggest city on Bali, a busy bustling place with cars, motor scooters and bicycles jostling with one another creating traffic with a little t.

Bali was a paradise in 1973, as it had tropical uncrowded beaches with little unobtrusive bungalows on the beach instead of miles of high-rise hotels like in Hawaii. Twice the size of Rhode Island, Bali lies roughly in the middle of Indonesia in the Indian Ocean with Borneo to the North and Australia to the South. The Balinese were friendly to us Western travelers, yet they kept their own rich and complete culture. They were proud of their unique way of life and wanted to share it with foreigners. Although Bali is a part of Indonesia and most Indonesians were Muslim, the Balinese followed a religion called Bali-Hinduism, which included ancient Balinese beliefs; they worshipped the spirits, ancestors, mountains and trees.

We had just one week to enjoy the paradise sung about in one of my favorite movies, "South Pacific", especially the song "Bali Hai." "Bali Hai will call you". And it did. We spent a few romantic days staying in one of the concrete block beach bungalows on Kuta Beach where we listened to the waves and the wind in the dancing palm trees. Feeling relaxed in this tropical warm paradise, Chris and I engaged in more lovemaking than usual. I thought it was a good time to bring up the possibility of trying to conceive. We were only ten days away from landing in New Zealand and I felt like throwing caution to the wind.

So, I began hesitantly in my tone, but straight to the point in my words, "Why don't we just cut out the condom?"

Chris was shocked as we hadn't discussed having children since our one and only brief conversation in San Francisco four years before and he said, "No, I think we should wait until we're settled in New Zealand and I have a job." Our lovemaking was curtailed and I was disappointed and mad at him for several hours, until he said, "I promise we'll start

Boy in rice paddy

baby-making when I have a job." I accepted his decision sadly and convinced myself that waiting until he had a job might be wise.

Walking on the beach, we watched a group of about thirty boys ranging in age from thirteen to eighteen practicing martial arts in the breaking surf. Strong, healthy, handsome bodies clothed in white cotton shirts and pants thrashed, kicked and punched the waves. They called out powerful commands and followed them with swift movements. Their spirit of youthful united energy and their fresh enthusiasm was exciting to watch. Their karate type movements looked like an exotic dance with the ocean.

The next day we discovered that there was an airline strike and very few planes were flying in and out of Bali. We felt angry at the inconvenience it might cause us as we had planned on leaving at the end of the week. We went to book a flight to Sydney and we were told to get on three waiting lists and to go "stand by" as all flights out of Bali were full. After some pondering, we went back to the flight desk and put our names on the three stand-by lists for the upcoming week-end.

The following morning we rented a Honda 100 and mapped out a three- day motorcycle trip around the island. We headed north out of the city, passing rice fields along the way. I had no idea how rice was grown since it had always come to me in a sealed plastic bag off the supermarket shelf. Though I saw the little plants growing in the rice ponds, I could not imagine the next steps of drying and getting millions of "ricelets" (a word I made up) into the plastic bags.

We spent our first night in the town of Ubud, considered "the art center" of Bali, which had one modest family-run hotel, a few restaurants and some shops. Ubud is home to many painters, woodcarvers and musicians. As we walked down the main street, Monkey Forest Road, we heard the Balinese traditional percussive gamelan music and saw a few long tailed, small, coffee colored, macaque monkeys. A sign in the restaurant where we ate said, "Don't feed our cute, mischievous monkeys as they may become aggressive." I gazed at the one sitting on a ceiling rafter eating the banana he had stolen from an Australian tourist. Paintings and woodcarvings were of Balinese myths, fables and tales of ancient ancestral spirits.

We heard about and signed up for the evening cultural program. On our way, we passed many women on their way to a holiday gathering at a village temple. With pot-luck dishes wrapped carefully in square woven baskets and piled on their heads, they smiled and giggled with one another perhaps talking about the dances, story-telling and music they were about to enjoy at their event.

At the cultural program for tourists, we were most impressed with the trance

dance. As a wise old woman chanted, dancers relaxed their bodies and went into a trance. Gods and goddesses entered the dancer's bodies causing them to dance wildly and make animal sounds until collapsing, at which point, the crone asked the gods to peacefully leave their bodies and the dancers awoke. The exotic music, costumes, headgear and wild movements of the dancers were otherworldly to me.

The following day, we stayed thirty miles north of Ubud in a place called Kintamani in the mountains where it was cooler. The women in the marketplace wore cardigan sweaters and towels wrapped around their shoulders as shawls over their western style blouses. They wore Balinese sarongs, a piece of Batik multicolored material wrapped around their waist. The mountain people of Bali looked very different than the people in the towns and main city. To me they looked removed with an inscrutable look in their eyes. They paid no attention to us.

These mountain people were said to be the true Balinese who were culturally isolated and practiced burial customs found nowhere else in Bali. According to the Bali-Hindu religion these Balinese let their dead decay slowly out in the open air; the birds eat the flesh and the skeletons are allowed to decompose and be of service to the other animals in the life cycle. The bodies are clothed when laid to rest inside a 3' bamboo structure called a "wadah". It is made flimsily so that the animals can

Mountain village of Kintamani

easily break it down and eat the flesh. We followed a self-proclaimed guide who beckoned us to take his canoe out on Lake Batur and over to the site where we saw the skeletons. Chris got up close and personal with his camera while I stood back, in awe of the reality of death.

I was frightened to see real skeletons with the eyes hollowed out; I pictured them in my mind for a few nights after. I was reminded how very afraid of death I was in my younger days. When my Grandpa died, I was twelve years old and there was an open casket. I glanced at him as I passed quickly by and saw his thick white hair and handsome face; he was dressed in a grey suit with a rose colored tie. He looked like he was sleeping, but I knew he was dead. My stomach was tight as I was anxious, but I shoved those feelings inside me because at that age I didn't understand them. The reason I didn't make it to my Grandma's funeral ten years later, was because the freaked out child came out again and made me so late that I arrived at our house when the relatives were all having coffee and cake, thus avoiding "the dead part." From the time my grandpa died and through college when I read Nietzche and took Philosophy, I had many nightmares about people dying and I'd wake suddenly in a sweat thinking, "I am going to die someday too." Marilyn Monroe committing suicide and James Dean's motorcycle accident appeared in my nightmares and always woke me with the frightful horror that I, Marcia, would also die.

Seeing the bodies burned in Benares (Veranasi) India and these Balinese dead people changed my perception of death. These two cultures believe in reincarnation and if I let myself believe I'd come back in another body, I'd be less afraid of death. I might even like it.

When we returned to the mountain village, the children flocked around our motorcycle, and they were keenly excited about having their picture taken. The snap of the camera may have made them feel included and complimented, I thought.

Temples were everywhere in Bali; triangular shaped thatched "rooflets" (another word I made up) piled one on top of the other with little square brick structures between them. Most people had a temple or shrine in their backyard.

On the third day, we found ourselves outside one such temple where an English speaking Balinese man came up to us and offered to be our guide. He wore the traditional Balinese sarong and a western style long sleeve shirt. He took us out on a circuitous path that led to the temple on the edge of a land spit with the ocean all around. There was a sign on the outside of the structure that read, "Attention - It's forbidden to enter, women during menstruation. Thanks." I did not have my period at the time, but I thought, "What if I did? How would they know?" I was too em-

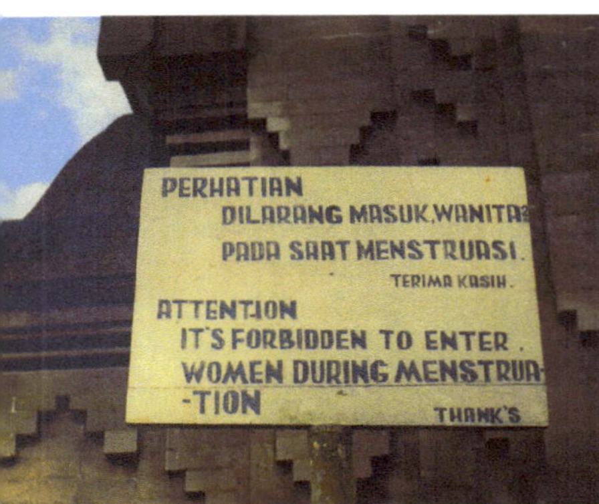
PERHATIAN
DILARANG MASUK.WANITA
PADA SAAT MENSTRUASI.
TERIMA KASIH.
ATTENTION
IT'S FORBIDDEN TO ENTER .
WOMEN DURING MENSTRUA-
-TION
THANK'S

barrassed to ask our guide why this was the rule. I imagined they thought we were unclean. I thought it the best time for a woman to enter a temple to pray, when her hormones were active and emotions raw.

As our guide told us about the temple, I noticed that he had five fingers and one thumb on his left hand. I had trouble listening to what he had to say as I kept counting his fingers to make sure I wasn't imagining this. He had a kind face, but I kept thinking sinister thoughts triggered by memories of the previous day's skeletons. I had already named him " Five Fingered Willy" while he was talking to us. I conjured up scary ghost stories told to me by the fire at summer camp. I kept nudging Chris to notice this phenomenon, but he kept talking to Five Fingered Willy and thanked him for the interesting tour while I was a bit shaken up for awhile.

When we were out of hearing distance, I said, "Didn't you see his five fingers?"

Chris replied, "What five fingers?"

Me stuck in the mud

I answered, "He had the normal four fingers and a thumb on his right hand, but on his left hand he had a thumb and five fingers. I continued, "His fifth finger came out just below his pinkie. I can't believe you didn't notice it since you are generally so observant. Didn't he seem monkeyish to you?"

Chris ruffled my hair affectionately and said," You're a monkey." I don't think he ever believed me.

The following day we got stuck in the mud on our way back to Denpasar. I laughed, while Chris was annoyed that the deluge of rain had slowed us down and was worried that the mud might have damaged the rented motorcycle, so we washed it and checked it carefully before returning it to the rental place. When I think of Bali, I think of the skeletons, which brought up early views of death, "Five Fingered Willy" and our motorcycle trip around the island.

In Denpasar, the day before we were to leave Bali, I worried about going "stand-by." All of a sudden I thought, "What if we couldn't get out? We'd be trapped in paradise." Would that be so bad? We'd been traveling for five months with only what fit in our packs and we were travel weary. I kept dreaming of one home, one bed, one toilet and one shower. And we were out of money. Though Bali was a beautiful paradise, I wanted out.

We checked out of our hotel in Denpasar at 11:00 AM and the proprietor was kind enough to hold our packs for pick-up later in the day. As we roamed around the market place picking up souvenirs and eating custard apples, I got more and more anxious about the possibility of not getting out of Bali that night. The waiting lists we were on were all Qantas flights leaving at 10:00 PM, 11:00 PM and 12:00 AM for Sydney. After our last Balinese dinner of Nasi Goreng, fried rice and vegetables with an egg scrambled in, we picked up our packs at the hotel and took a bus out to the airport arriving around 8:00 PM We made sure our names were still on the three waiting lists before settling into the take-off zone with the other passengers. At 9:00 PM the names of the few people who would go stand-by for the 10 o'clock flight were called. They were not our names. Chris, who often looked at things negatively, and me, who often looked at things positively, switched our thinking styles.

I was surprised Chris was not worried, as he said, "We'll probably get called for the 11:00 o'clock flight."

I, on the other hand, said, with anxiety mounting in my voice, "But supposing we're not called at all? Will we sleep in the airport, or go back to our old hotel, or try to get a room in another hotel nearer to the airport?"

Chris replied, "Let's play another round of chess." We carried this tiny four inch fold up plastic chess set with magnetic pieces which saved the day during times of waiting for transport in all the many airports and train stations on our trip. Chess playing was always one of our enjoyable activities. If Chris won he felt radiant and if I won he was pleased that he had married a brilliant woman.

At 10:00 PM the stand-by names were called and again we were not the chosen ones. My frustration mounted and I had a bad taste in my mouth, literally, from some rancid ghee. I really didn't want to spend one more day in Bali. Another round of chess, then at 11:00 PM the stand-by names were called out by the flight attendant, "Christian and Marcia Heinegg."

Excited and relieved we walked up to the plane entryway, accepted our boarding passes, and skipped on to the plane leaving paradise behind.

Postscript: We started attempting to conceive when Chris got a job a few months later...but it took four long years before I became pregnant.

Nasi Goreng

(Indonesian Fried Rice)

1 cup rice
2 tbsp. sesame oil
1/2 chili
2 cloves garlic
3 green onions
¼ cabbage
6 med. Shrimp
1 egg
½ tsp salt
1 tbsp. sweet soy sauce
¼ cucumber
1 small tomato

Cook rice as per package directions, fluff and set aside. Chop green onions. Slice garlic. Finely chop chili. Shred cabbage. Fry ingredients in wok with oil. Add shrimp and salt. Separately scramble egg in bowl and then make thin omelette. Cut egg in strips and toss into wok. Add rice and mix. Add soy sauce. Slice cucumber and tomato into strips and garnish on top of mixture.

This dish is tasty, but don't use purple cabbage as I did, because it turned the shrimp purple.

Criminals in Sydney

Our Qantas jet bounced on the tarmac of the Sydney Airport like the kangaroo imprinted on the side of the plane. I wondered if this last weekend before arriving in New Zealand would be a bumpy one. We hadn't slept at all well curled up in those straight-backed airplane seats. The ride from Bali to Sydney had been eight hours long. It only looked like 1/2 inch on the map.

We got our packs off the baggage turnstile and waited in line to go through customs. I was delighted to see everything written in English. We had been in foreign speaking third world countries now for five months. I kept wondering, "Where are the second world countries?"

When the people ahead of us had walked on, we approached the Custom's officer.

He barked, "Step behind the red line until you are called." We did as we were told. A moment later, he beckoned with his hand to step up. We presented our passports.

He glanced through them and said, "Where's your visa?"

Chris answered, "We were told we didn't need a visa if we were staying less then seventy-two hours so that's what we planned to do." Chris explained that we would be traveling onto New Zealand after a brief weekend visit with my relatives.

The Custom's official said, "Who do you think you are coming to our country without a visa?" I was completely intimidated by this guy and let Chris handle it. I could see Chris's ire rush to his cheeks with a red flush.

But Chris calmly responded, "We requested travel information from your embassy in Washington D.C. and in small print it said that one did not need a visa if one stayed only seventy-two hours."

The officer then barked, "Stand over there." He began taking other passengers standing in line. Weary, we stood by our packs and waited about twenty minutes. Then Chris stepped forward to inquire about our status.

The official said, “I’ve summoned another officer to question you.” We waited another ten minutes.

A second blond, athletic looking officer, who smelled of Brille Creme approached us wearing a light blue short sleeve shirt and navy blue shorts with navy knee socks and said, “Follow me.” He walked several steps ahead of us. We followed him down several long airport corridors and finally into an office.

He lit a cigarette, blew the smoke out of his nose, inhaled and then shouted at us, “You cannot enter Australia without a visa. You must purchase a ticket and get on the next plane to New Zealand.”

I then piped up, “But I want to visit my cousin who lives in Sydney and then we’ll be off to New Zealand in seventy-two hours.” He stomped off muttering that he was booking us an immediate flight to Wellington, New Zealand. I started frantically rustling in my pack and produced some papers from the Australian embassy in Washington D.C. that showed the tiny part about the seventy-two hours. It did say that one needed to have purchased a ticket onward prior to entry and we had not done so.

The man returned with two tickets on a plane leaving for Wellington in two hours. I showed him the paper from his embassy and read it aloud. He said, “This is no longer valid and you did not enter with an onward ticket. How do we know you will not become an “overstayer”?” I had not heard this term before, which meant, people who overstayed their visa expiration date. Australia had a strict immigration policy and overstaying was a problem.

I said, “ Couldn’t I just call my relative?”

He replied, “Sure, be my guest”, now in a gracious tone, as he pushed his desk phone towards me. I shuffled around in my pack for the phone number and dialed it. To my luck, my mother’s first cousin, Trude, answered the phone and I explained the situation.

She said, “Let me talk to the customs officer.” I handed the phone to him and he spoke very politely to her. She convinced him that she personally would get us on a plane in seventy-two hours. By the grace of God, the custom’s officer relented.

He took the name and address of my cousin and told her to report to him personally on Monday Jan.16th. Then he re-issued new tickets for that day, and let us go with “I’ll see you in my office in seventy-two hours.”

As we scampered away, Chris said, soto voce, “What a fucking Nazi Kangaroo.”

Seething with the same level of anger I retorted, “Bloody officious bastard.” Tired but determined to get to Trude and Joe’s place, we took the airport bus to Sydney central and a train out to their suburb.

That comment, “I’ll see you in my office,” rankled Chris and reminded him of his school days in the fifties in New Zealand when corporal punishment was the rule. As the subway rattled on, Chris ranted, “Most schools used the cane, but my school used the strap. I remember this male teacher taking off his belt and strapping with one hand while holding his pants up with the other. Most teachers kept a special strap for this purpose in their drawer.”

I asked, “How old were you?”

Chris responded, “I was eleven or twelve, it was in Johnsonville, a working class suburb of Wellington. It would have been standard five.” I later learned that was equivalent to seventh grade in the USA.

I asked, “Were you strapped?”

Chris said, “Yes, I was told to come up to the front of the room and put out my hand, then I got three or four whacks across my palm with his belt.”

“That must have hurt quite a bit.”

“Righty ho. It was a burning feeling that would last a half hour. My hand was red and stinging. I couldn’t use my hand, but I think they strapped the non-dominant hand so that you could still write.” I looked out the window and saw rows and rows of warehouses of Foster’s beer, one of Australia’s best.

“What did you do to get this punishment?”

“Oh, anything that annoyed the teacher; talking in class, not paying attention, passing notes.”

“And what about the cane?”

“It was a proper wooden paddle. Boys who were sent to the office were asked to bend over and they got maybe as many as fifteen hard whacks on the buttocks.”

“Ouch.”

“The saying goes...”An occasional pat on the back does a kid good as long as it is low enough and hard enough.”

Suburban ticky-tacky houses like those in Daly City whizzed by as the train clanked on towards our stop on the outskirts of Sydney.

Chris said, “Remind me how Trude is related to you.”

“Trude is my mother’s first cousin which makes her my first cousin once removed.”

Chris looked puzzled and asked, “Once removed to where?”

“Once removed a generation.”

“Why would you remove a whole generation?”

“We’re not removing a generation; it’s genealogical terminology. Trude’s mother, Molly, and my mother’s mother, Sida, were sisters. Then Molly and Sida’s daughters: Trude and Taube are in the same generation. I am in the next generation so I am Trude’s first cousin once removed a generation. Get it?"

Chris gave me a confused smile and looked out the window.

Trude was in her fifties when we visited her in Sydney and was married to her second husband, Joe. Gadi was her eighteen-year-old son from her previous marriage and he lived in Sydney with them. I had met Trude and Gadi the summer I was fifteen, when I visited Israel with a youth group from my temple. She and her first husband lived in Haifa with their ten-year-old son and their new baby, Gadi.

To give Chris a little more background, I told about how when Trude was twelve years old, she and her younger brother lived with their parents in Vienna, Austria. In 1944, the children were put on the Kindertransport train, which took Jewish children out of Austria. Her parents were to follow, but they were taken to the concentration camp, Theresienstadt, and she never saw them again.

Trude grew up in a foster Jewish family in London. At the age of twenty, she married an English Jewish soldier, named Walter, who moved her to the new state of Israel. Many years later Trude and Walter divorced. A few years after that Joe, a Polish Jew who was a Holocaust survivor and who had immigrated to Australia was visiting Israel and he met Trude. They fell in love, married and he moved her and her second son, Gadi, to Sydney, Australia.

From the train stop, we walked a few blocks to Trude and Joe's apartment. Trude greeted us like we were long lost family, and we were. She was warm and huggable and felt like family to me. She looked like my mother and my aunties and after five months of travel I felt the need of familiarity. She gave big bosom-to-bosom hugs. The apartment smelled of chicken soup and a popular Israeli love song, Erev Ba, played on the record player.

Joe was lively and jovial, entertaining us with stories of his adventures. Though he mentioned very briefly how he got to Australia through various refugee camps and miles of immigration papers, he specified nothing about his life in a concentration camp or how he survived it. Although I was curious about what it was like for him in the concentration camp, I knew he didn't want the conversation to go in that direction. The numbers on his arm were apparent but I think he was so grateful to be alive and to be with the lovely Trude that he lived each day enjoying and appreciating the moment.

The only thing I remember about eighteen year old Gadi, was his unique accent – a mixture of guttural Hebrew and Australian. It was funny and it made me laugh. Chris and Gadi played chess. Throughout the weekend we all joked about the officious characters at the airport repeating the line, "I'll see you in my office." We slept

much of the seventy-two hours recovering from jet lag but managed one tourist outing to the Sydney Opera House – a stunning piece of architecture! We enjoyed our visit with Trude and her family and we made our New Zealand flight within the seventy-two hour limit, but Australia made me feel like a bad child, slightly criminal.

Jewish Chicken Soup

1 whole chicken
1 onion
2-3 stalks of celery
3-4 carrots
1 parsnip
2 cloves garlic
1 bay leaf
salt & pepper

Put the chicken in a large soup pot and fill with water to cover. Add in chopped onion, celery, garlic and bay leaf. Bring to a boil then lower the flame to low and cook covered for 2 hours. Check water level every ½ hour and add more water to cover. Skim off fat. After 2 hours pull the chicken out and put on plate to cool. Add the sliced carrots, parsnip and celery. Pull the fat off and discard then pull the meat off the bones and return half the chicken torn into smaller pieces back into the soup. Season with salt and pepper. Optional: add rice or noodles.

Ah ! The aroma of this soup nourishes body, mind and soul.

Postscript: Over the years, we never wanted to go back to Australia when we visited New Zealand to see Chris's parents. But in 2006 we decided to visit some New Zealand friends who had moved to Sydney. It had been thirty years and we planned to be in New Zealand to attend a memorial of one of our oldest and dearest friends. Hoping over to Australia would only be a further three-hour plane ride.

Our Sydney friends showed us the sights of their city by ferry boat. Chris hopped onto the ferry taxi, but left one foot on shore as he told the ferry captain that his wife was just running up to make this ferry and could he please wait one more minute.

The ferry captain shouted, "Take your foot off the dock, that's against safety regulations," just as I jumped onto the ferry. Criminals again.

Next stop: New Zealand!

The End?

The end for now. A sequel covering our three and a half years living in New Zealand will follow.

www.ingramcontent.com/pod-product-compliance
Lightning Source LLC
LaVergne TN
LVHW070129110826
845147LV00002B/220

* 9 7 8 0 5 7 8 0 0 1 4 3 2 *